MW00899757

ADULTING LIKE A PRO

Essential Life Skills for Teens and Young Adults, and Tips on How to Become a Grown-up. With an Activity After Every Chapter.

MIRANDA YOUNG

TABLE OF CONTENTS

Get this collection of ten activities in a printable PDF that is easy to use.

Download now and kickstart your adulting journey.

Simply follow this link, or scan the QR code, and you will get:

- All ten exercises found in the book in a printable PDF form for ease of use.
- Updates on any future releases
- Special discounts on upcoming releases.

https://book.essentiallifeskills.pro/

Miranda Young

INTRODUCTION

You wake up one day, usually on your eighteenth birthday, and suddenly it's official, you're an adult. Apart from the usual birthday excitement, you don't look or feel any different. So, what's changed? What does it mean to become an adult?

When we refer to the word *adult*, it means you've reached a specific time in your life when you're expected to be more responsible. As you're effectively a grown-up, you are expected to display certain characteristics expected of an adult, such as managing your finances, taking control of your own life, and taking care of yourself. The thing is, we don't just wake up on our 18th and suddenly start acting like an adult. Some people may not even know how to effectively be an adult, because nobody shows you. But don't worry, there are some basic life skills and hacks you can learn to help you be a successful young adult. This book will help you transition with confidence and independence, as you embark on your journey into adulthood.

It's time to learn how to adult like a pro!

If you're ready to learn how to be successful at work, the basics of managing your finances, buying your first car or home, and what you'll need to make this possible, this book is ideal for you.

If you want to be more productive and need help developing a daily routine and a plan for self-development and growth, this book is for you—even adults need "me" time.

If you want to stay focused on your career and are ready to ace your job applications, succeed in interviews, and gain promotions by developing your soft skills, keep reading!

I know what it's like to make that journey into adulthood alone, with very little guidance, because it's just assumed that you're an adult and you'll figure it out. While I did, I would have really benefited from some help and guidance along the way, as I didn't want to ask my parents for their advice, help, or assistance—I wanted to prove I could do this. But that doesn't mean I didn't need direction, as there were so many things I wish I'd known first, which would've made life so much easier.

I wrote this book because I have so much valuable information to share with you, which will make your transition into adulthood fun and easy. In fact, fun is a huge part of being an adult. I want you to enjoy your journey and make your own informed choices and good decisions along the way, which shape who you are. There's so much I've learned and so much I wish I'd known as I headed into adulthood, and I want to share this as a reflection of my own experience.

In the following chapters, I'm about to share with you:

- The skills you need as an adult, in order to satisfy your basic needs.
- The responsibilities you need to take on when living in your own home.

- Basic financial advice that will keep you moving steadily along and help you maximize your finances—I don't want you to struggle!
- The benefits of setting up a daily routine and positive environment that ensure you're as organized and productive as possible.
- How you can find the perfect job and perform well in your interview.
- How you can succeed at work, so you can progress and excel in your career.

Imagine how proud you'll feel, knowing all this stuff without having to ask your parents. I bet they'll be impressed because taking ownership of your life is an act of adulting.

You have so much to look forward to as you head into adulthood, but you are in control of your future. There's no need to feel overwhelmed or pressured when it comes to adulthood, because you're not doing this alone—we're doing this together. This book is your guide toward a successful adult life and is here to help you take control and forge your own path.

Many of the things you need to know aren't taught in high school or even college, which means the skills and knowledge you need for day-to-day life aren't always obvious. You are about to secure your future by learning crucial skills that will help you lead a healthy, successful, and fulfilling life—you can start your adult life by putting your best foot forward!

We'll start off by talking about your passions, because this is your life, so what you want and feel passionate about is important. Let's talk about it in Chapter 1.

The purpose of our lives is to be happy.

–DALAI LAMA

CHAPTER 1

Finding Your Passions

Passion is energy. Feel the power that comes from focusing on what excites you.

– OPRAH WINFREY

An important part of being an adult is choosing the life you want. Every adult should be leading a fulfilled and happy life that ultimately heads toward the life they want and deserve. While the idea of becoming an adult may sometimes seem daunting or boring, it's important to recognize that being an adult can also be fun. It's an exciting time in your life when you can take the reins—your future is in your hands.

But what is that future and what does it look like?

That's what you need to figure out, because everyone envisions their life differently. You need to think about your passions in life, what you'll do for fun, what job you want, and what you want your life to look like. In order to do that, you should start to identify the things you're passionate about in life, and that's what we'll focus on in this chapter.

You'll focus on your life's purpose, figuring out the things you love to do, and how you can use your passions to spark your motivation. You'll also compare your hobbies to your career hopes, and we'll discuss the possibilities for a side hustle and its potential to become a fully functional business, with the opportunity for growth.

I want you to enjoy your life and feel excited about it so you can be proactive. You can then start to take purposeful steps toward getting that life.

What's Your Purpose in Life?

Wow! This sounds like a really out-there question that you may never have thought about, but it's not as complicated as you might think. You may have heard many people talk about figuring out their "why." Basically, your "why" is your life's purpose. Over time, your life's purpose can evolve, so don't worry, you're not signing a legal contract by trying to figure this out now. It does, however, help you direct and shape your life.

When you know your purpose, you become more capable of pursuing the things in life that give you the most fulfillment. This purpose is your anchor; it becomes the thing you return to when taking action or making decisions in your life, as it keeps you focused on your goals. It helps you be clear in relation to your life goals and, therefore, allows you to monitor your progress as you strive towards achieving your purpose. It helps you develop your resilience, because with it, you're more likely to overcome any barriers that stand in your way, while maintaining your integrity. In 2010, a study conducted by *Applied*

Psychology found that people who have a sense of purpose and control, and feel like what they do is worthwhile, often tend to live longer. This is thought to be because they take more care of their own health and well-being (Morin, 2020).

Working Out Your Purpose

Once you figure out your purpose in life, you'll be able to make plans for your immediate and long-term future. To start working out your purpose, you should:

1. Find out what drives you. Close your eyes, take a deep breath, and envision your ideal life. Ask yourself the questions below to help you figure this out:

   a. What makes you feel happy?
   b. What makes you feel proud?
   c. When you do something, who do you do it for?
   d. What is important to you in life?
   e. If you had only a year to do everything you wanted to do, what would you do?

2. Use your vision of your life and your purpose to create a vision board or collage of the things you want in life. If you want to be able to take plenty of vacations, find an image that represents that. Find an image that represents the house of your dreams, your career, your financial situation, your family, and anything else you love. Include your hobbies, too, and if you can't find images, write or type out the words in a decorative or creative way. There are two options for your vision board or collage:

ADULTING LIKE A PRO

    a.   Create a digital vision board or collage on a device, such as a laptop or a tablet.

    b.   Create a physical vision board, using images that you cut out and stick on, as well as colored pens, pencils, or markers.

3. Create your top three life goals. For instance, if you want to have a healthy and happy life, you can then break down your goals into smaller steps that help you get this happy and healthy life that you dream of. This all depends on what a happy and healthy life means for you. You can then detail steps to help you get there. If your career plays an important part in that, you can detail that you need to finish school, get your college degree, what training you need to do, and what jobs you need to do to reach your target.

Don't forget to display your vision board and goals in a place that ensures you see them daily. You need to be reminded of them every day!

Now that you've completed this exercise, you'll understand a little more about what you want in life. You should regularly revisit this exercise, because even when we're an adult, our needs and wants tend to change over time, which means our goals change too, and that's okay. They should change, because as we journey through life, we change too!

Let's move on and talk about your passion.

08

Figuring Out Your Passions

When you're passionate about something, you're devoted to a particular task, thing, or concept, because you like it or it's desirable to you. You tend to pursue your passions because they appeal to you and inspire you.

Think about your week:

- What high points have you experienced?
- What things were you excited about?
- What was the best part of each day?
- What did you spend your money on?
- How did you spend your time?
- What did you enjoy talking about?
- What did you do particularly well, or what are you good at?
- What did you look forward to?

When you've answered these questions, explore each of your answers further and consider how each of these things inspires you. Your passions can help you identify the skills you have that you are good at and enjoy. For example, if you enjoy spending social time with friends and family, you need to consider why. Maybe it's because you're a people person or a good communicator, which are excellent, transferable skills that will serve you throughout your life.

Passion Leads to Motivation

If you're struggling to find your passions, you could try:

1. Writing lists of the things that are important to you.
2. Brain-dumping the activities you enjoy or look forward to.
3. Asking others what they think you're good at and why.

When you know what your passions are, you can use them to motivate yourself. Self-motivation is important for all adults, as it helps you to succeed. We've already discussed setting goals and breaking down goals briefly in the earlier section. If you know what you're passionate about and your purpose, you can use these things to tap into your motivation, as they're your incentives.

Let's say you have a list of things you need to do, such as a homework assignment. You may be putting off doing it; however, you take a look at your vision board and life goals to remind yourself of the things you really want in life. Completing your school education plays a part in this, so you need to reframe how you're thinking.

Say it with enthusiasm:

I need to complete this assignment, so I can get the grades at school I need, to get into the college I want, get my degree, and get the life I desire.

Don't just say it, believe it, because you know it's true. You can have the life you desire, but you have to take action toward your goals. This form of driving your emotion is rewarding and you'll feel satisfied working towards this. As you're heading for long-term goals, it's important that you don't lose focus—waiting for your future reward isn't always easy.

If we enjoy doing something, it often seems like a reward in itself, but we don't enjoy everything we do. If you find that something you have to do is difficult, but it contributes toward your future goals, you can use other forms of rewards to help motivate you. Rewards often encourage us to achieve our short-term goals (such as completing an assignment).

Let's say you're doing a math assignment, but you hate math. You could offer yourself a suitable reward. If I get my assignment done, I can:

- spend time playing video games
- invite my friends over
- go and hang out with my friends
- have a treat—some candy, a specialty coffee, or something new from the mall
- head to the movies with my mom.

Think

Think about the things you need to do. Transform your to-do items into goals. If there's something you don't feel motivated to do, make a note of how you can motivate yourself to do it.

You've done some great self-exploration so far. You know your purpose, your passions, and what motivates you. It's time to start focusing on getting the balance right between your hobby and your career.

Hobby Versus Career

Sometimes, our hobby becomes our career, so it can be quite difficult to tell the difference between the two. A hobby is something you do for fun, at your leisure. It's usually an activity you like, such as reading, sewing or stitching, crafting, playing a sport (for fun), gardening, drawing or painting, or even dancing or writing.

Your career is generally your job journey or plan, and it's often something you are passionate about. It refers to your chosen profession, trade, vocation, or occupation, but it can also refer to how you got there. For instance, if you want to progress into a manager or director role at an IT company, you may need to start in an entry-level IT role first, progressing through training, education, gaining experience and obtaining several promotions, before you finally get to a management or director position.

We usually aren't paid to complete our hobbies, but when it comes to our careers, we are paid for the job we do. A career is usually something that you have to nurture and cultivate, and it often requires you to make sacrifices. For example, if you want a senior position, you may need to study for a management qualification in your own time, outside of work, and you may even need to pay for that yourself. You're therefore sacrificing your time and investing money to get better job opportunities.

Our hobbies are usually things we enjoy doing, but you might not enjoy everything you have to do in your job or career; however, money is the motivating factor here. It's important to get the right balance between your career and your hobbies, so if you enjoy playing video games, there's no reason why you can't still do that as an adult. Maybe you have a little time in the evening or on a weekend. Our hobbies allow us downtime, so it's important to ensure you still make time for them, as well as your career.

While it's okay not to like certain aspects of your job, it's important that you like your career, or where your career is going, because if you hate it, it won't serve you in the long term and it will eventually impact your performance and happiness.

> *The only way to do great work is to love what you do.*
>
> –STEVE JOBS

It's important to be able to combine your career and aspects of your hobbies, to get the right balance. But you might be wondering, *how can I get the balance right*?

To do this, you should:

- Make a list of your hobbies and think about why you like each one. You've already done this when we discussed your purpose and passions, so now all you have to do is incorporate your hobbies too.
- Consider what skills and qualities you need to utilize or embrace as part of your hobbies.
- When you look at your hobbies, are there any opportunities to make money?

- Are there any skills you use when carrying out your hobbies that you can also carry over into your career?

For instance, if you like gardening, you could make money by offering to work on some of your neighbors' gardens. If you like looking after kids, you could start babysitting.

If you earn a part-time income when you're still studying or working full-time, this is usually called a side hustle.

Considering a Side Hustle?

A side hustle is a great way to earn extra money outside of your education or full-time job. It can provide you with the opportunity to try out different career paths too. When you consider a side hustle, you should look at doing something that allows you to use your skills and interests, as well as linking to your professional goals. For example, if you're good at English and are interested in a career in education, you could start tutoring middle school kids, who are struggling with the topic. If you're a dancer, you could ask around at the local dance schools to see if they'll hire you to teach a class.

In this chapter so far, we've talked about figuring out your purpose and your passions, and we've even talked about your hobbies and motivation. If you can turn these passions into a side hustle, you can make extra money or, sometimes, turn it into a full-time business.

You're probably wondering why we're talking about side hustles but it's because they are great if you want to grow your skills—helping you become job-ready. Running a side hustle provides you with flexibility, as you do this in your spare time or work it around your other commitments. It can also help you to explore your passions and provide you with a very enjoyable job, as well as improve your finances, because you'll be bringing in extra income.

The top 10 side hustles for teens and young adults include:

1. social media influencer
2. social media manager
3. affiliate marketer
4. dog walker
5. tutor—online or in-person
6. lawnmower or gardener
7. selling digital products or services you've created (website design, e-books, courses)
8. car washer
9. online writer (travel writer and product reviews)
10. newspaper deliverer

But there's no reason why you can't embrace other talents of yours too. If you have a knack for tech, maybe you could help older people in your area install their technology, set it up, and show them how to use it. Others offer ironing and cleaning services, while others are good at crafting, baking, or candle-making, so they make their own products. You can certainly make money from your writing too—you could write YouTube video scripts, books, and articles, or you could even start your own blog, which can also be monetized. AI is currently changing how we're working and ChatGPT is creating a buzz because it's so new and exciting. This is a bot that is programmed in language and is able to string words together—basically it writes fresh content for you! People who know how to use this effectively are highly sought-after right now.

But what happens if your side hustle is a total success, and you want to turn this into a full-time business?

Turning a Side Hustle into a Business

Sometimes, a side hustle becomes a viable business idea that allows you to make a full-time income. If you enjoy your side hustle, and it's pretty successful, you can test it to see if you could make a good level of income from it.

Usually, the decision to turn a side hustle into a full-time business is based on how much money you think you can make from it. Adults have financial responsibilities, and when you are just starting to form your career, you need to ensure there's room to grow your business.

If your side hustle is going well, start by listing the products or services you offer. Then consider how much money you need to earn each month and create a financial goal. Work out how many of your products/services you would need to sell, in order to reach your monthly financial goal. You can even do this when you first start out with your side hustle, as it gives you a goal to focus on.

You then need to consider how realistic this is—do you think you can meet this financial goal? Do you have enough time to go all in and do this full-time? You also need to think about how many new customers you would need to get, in order to make the business viable.

For example, let's say you're gardening for people on your block. You can only do so many gardens each day, so there's only so much you can earn each week. Sometimes, your customers may tell you to skip their garden this week, or the weather may stop you from being able to carry out your duties. On the days you don't earn money, you need to account for this and be smart. Your job may be more prosperous over the spring and summer; however, you can still only work on so many gardens each day. You would have to work out how many gardens you can do and allow for people who don't want their gardens to be done every week or month. That means you may need to look for some extra products and services to bring in extra income, as one product or service often isn't enough, especially if you plan on growing your business.

Business growth often means you add extra products or services to your business, or you change the way you work. It can also mean you start to take on employees, buy tools, equipment, or technology that helps you do your job quicker, or you increase your prices.

Let's stay with the gardener example and consider growth and subsequent income ideas:

- You could write a book with a gardening topic.
- You could start an e-store, selling gardening-related items.
- You could sell add-on sales to your customers, such as plants, grass feed, repellents, seeds and bulbs, bird feeders, and information sheets on garden care topics.
- You could even teach gardening to groups of people. This way, you can serve more than one customer at the same time.

- You could employ someone and pay them a salary so they can do some of the work.
- You could buy new gardening equipment and tools so you can speed up the time it takes you to work. For example, a ride-on lawnmower may take half the time a push-along mower does.
- You could raise your prices.
- You could start an online gardening membership that offers discounted products and services in your store or through affiliate links, along with explainer videos, and gardening tips and advice.
- You could recommend and review online gardening products and equipment and refer your audience to them via an affiliate link. An affiliate link is when you recommend products and services that belong to other people, such as Amazon, and you get a commission for selling their products when a person buys them. You simply have to sign up with companies that offer an affiliate plan, and then generate links that prove a person bought the item because of you.

As you can see from this example, there are many ways to grow a business and make money. The way you grow your business depends on what type of business you're running. The best thing to consider for growth purposes is thinking of ways to serve more customers, and often, this means creating a course, teaching groups, writing books, or creating products, such as subscription boxes, or employing staff.

The time to grow your business is when you're earning as much money as you can and it's impossible for you to earn any more, without changing the way you work. This is often referred to as "hitting the income ceiling", because you've hit the maximum amount of money you can for the hours you're working and, therefore, you have to look for ways to earn more money that don't take up any more of your time.

To do this, you have to think outside the box—but that's the same with any business!

Activity #1: Your Side Hustle Business Model

While you may still be young, you know a lot and have earned so much. It's possible to turn any of these things into a side hustle, and it's time you thought about that.

- Write a list of all the things you know, have qualifications in, or have experience in.
- Sort your list—Highlight everything you've listed that you enjoy doing (think about those things you're passionate about).
- Choose your top three–how could you turn them into a side hustle?
- Brain-dump how you can make money from each of these ideas. Can you teach it and create another product or service?

Knowing the products and services you're going to offer is the start of your business model. To continue with this, you need to know how much you need to earn from each product or service. This then allows you to forecast (guess with reasonable accuracy) how much you believe you can earn each month and in your first year.

Once you have that information, you can start to consider whom you will sell your products and services to. Most people begin a side hustle because it's something they enjoy doing, and often they end up with customers by accident, but there is a market out there for your product or service. In order for your side hustle to become a business, you need to know who your customers are.

Figuring out the things you're passionate about and good at can help you shape your future career. Earning an extra income from your side hustle will also give you the opportunity to save money and build good money habits. We'll talk about this later in Chapter 3. Next, we'll talk about finding your own place to live. This is another thing that you'll need money for, when you're a young adult.

CHAPTER 2

Finding Your Own Place and Making it Your Home

There's no place like home.

– L. FRANK BAUM

When you're a young adult and you begin looking for a place to live, it's often expected that you'll automatically know what to do, but this isn't the case. There are so many things to consider, because not only are you responsible for the place you live, but you also want to be comfortable there too.

In this chapter, we're going to explore how to choose your first apartment, set up your utilities, and other things you may need, such as the internet. We'll also talk through some fire safety tips in the home, furnishing your home, and we'll also talk through some tips to help you keep your place clean and tidy. As an extra, we'll also talk about decluttering and what you should consider if you want a pet.

By the end of this chapter, you'll be able to choose your first place and move in with confidence.

Choosing an Apartment

It's exciting when you're searching for your first home. You have lots of decisions to make, depending on your budget, but you'll find that you receive a lot of information too. It's important that you take an objective view, so you can come to your own decisions.

We'll talk about buying your first home in Chapter 9, but when it comes to viewing the property, the concepts are really similar. For the purposes of this Chapter, we'll be focusing on renting.

Renting a property means you move into a place you call your own, but it actually belongs to someone else. This person is your landlord. You then pay them rent to live there.

Typically, you pay your rent on a monthly basis for an agreed period. This is usually for 6–12 months, although you and your landlord can extend this when the term ends, provided you are both happy with the agreement.

You should make sure that you always:

- Choose a location that meets your needs. Think of the places you need to commute to (work, visiting family, or school), and how accessible this is. If you are quite a distance away, consider transportation or travel costs you may have to pay.
- Research the neighborhood you're considering residing in. You may want to consider crime in the area, along with other statistics, such as average rent costs. You should also look at what amenities are available in this area too.

When viewing properties, there are so many things you should consider.

- Take a good look at the outside of the property to see if it looks well-maintained and in good repair. Paintwork will peel if it's old, and you should also look at any outdoor spaces and the immediate surroundings, as this will give you an indication of the area.

- You should do the same when inside the property; however, some things can be fixed with a little bit of paint.

- Don't allow low rent alone to persuade you; ensure you check for damp patches and mold. If the windows have much condensation, there's a funny musty smell, or the wallpaper is peeling in some areas, this could be an indication of dampness.

- Be sure to check the bathroom thoroughly, as sometimes the fixtures and fittings aren't maintained well in rental properties.

- Turn on the faucets to see if they flow well and to check there are no leaks. A bathroom is also a common place for dampness and mold.

- If you're considering a house, test the lights to ensure the electric works well.

- Consider the security of the house, including all doors and windows. An entrance door usually has at least two locks, and windows need to be lockable but also able to be used as possible escape routes.

- Some people also check their cell reception—it's a nightmare when you can't use your cell phone at your home.

- Take a quiet moment to assess the noises around the apartment. Listen out for neighbors, traffic, footsteps, etc, to see if it's going to be too noisy for you.
- Look for storage space, such as cabinets and closets.
- Imagine your own things in this place—can you envision this being your home?

Make sure you come back and view the place again, if it's on your list as a possible rental, and don't be afraid to ask the right questions. Ask questions like:

- Do you have certificates or paperwork for maintenance and safety checks in the property?
- What's the neighborhood like?
- Am I able to decorate this to a style I like, or are there any rules regarding décor?
- Are there any security devices, such as CCTV or burglar alarms installed on the property?
- What internet provider serves the property?
- Are there any noise issues in the area?
- How should the rent be paid, what's the total cost, and when does it need to be paid?
- Are there any other costs you expect prior to moving in? Most places require a security deposit, bond, or rent advance, so double-check how much this is first.
- Which utilities will I be responsible for? Some rental agents cover certain utilities like electric or heat within the rental price.
- If I have an emergency, who do I contact?

- Who is responsible for maintaining the outdoor space?

It's a good idea to write a list of questions before you view the property, and that way, if you have any specific queries, you'll remember to ask everything you need to know.

Before you move into a property, you're expected to sign a contract to agree to the terms of your tenancy (how long you'll live there, confirming you'll keep it in good condition, agreeing to pay the rent on time, what notice period you'll give if you decide to leave the property, and how much rent you'll pay). Be sure to read through this carefully, and if you're not sure of something, ask questions or seek legal advice if necessary.

Look over the section that talks about costs and check that the monthly rent is what you've agreed upon, and also read the information about security deposits. Your deposit is usually a double rent payment—so you pay your deposit, along with a month's rent in advance. When you pay a security deposit for a property, this is usually returned to you when you leave, provided you've kept the property in good condition, have paid your rent on time, and haven't broken any other rules. The information about when you will receive your deposit back is usually detailed in your contract too. Sometimes, a contract is referred to as a lease agreement.

Remember, a contract is a legal document, so you should read through everything carefully before signing.

Once you've chosen a home or apartment to rent, signed the contract, and received your keys, you're ready to go. But what else do you need to pay for?

What Else Do I Need to Set Up, Arrange, or Pay For?

Sometimes, some of your utilities are included with your rent, especially if you're renting an apartment or room in student accommodation. Make sure you are clear on what utilities are included, as some things you need to pay for may include:

- water
- heat
- electricity
- internet
- parking
- cleaning (in communal areas)

It's really important to find the most cost-effective and reliable internet, electricity, and heat providers. Shop around for the best offer and service that meets your needs. You can ask for some information from your landlord and you can even compare prices online.

On top of this, you will have your personal living costs to cover, such as food, toiletries, cosmetics, and clothing. When working out how much you have to spend on a rental property, you should consider all of your expenses (in the list above), to ensure you can afford your own place.

When you are looking for your first rental, you should consider if you want to rent alone, or share with a friend. This can reduce your costs by half in some cases and renting a home can be really expensive. Even though you have several costs to pay, in addition to your rental costs, it's really important to ensure you choose the right person to share a home with—someone you can actually live with, as you know and trust them. You're going to be tied in an agreement with them for several months, possibly even a year, so you have to be as sure as you can be that things will work out.

We'll talk more about money in Chapter 3, so you can learn key budgeting skills in time for you to get your own place. Next, we're touching on some simple fire safety tips, and although personal safety is something we'll talk about later in this book, fire safety is super important when you move into your first place.

Tips for Fire Safety in the Home

When you move into a rental property, you should ensure there are carbon monoxide detectors and fire alarms inside the space. You should check that they are fully functioning and speak to your landlord about their condition—how old are they, for instance? Typically, your landlord will have these checked on a yearly basis.

Fire is a real risk in your home, so don't underestimate the risk. Some basic fire safety includes:

- When you're cooking, concentrate on cooking and don't get distracted.

- Unplug electrical items when you're not using them.

- Never put your laundry on at night and then go to bed; do it when you're awake and on the property.

- If you use candles, keep them at least 12 inches away from anything flammable. If you go out or to bed, blow them out first.

It's good practice to have a simple fire escape plan, so you know what to do, just in case a fire emergency occurs. To create your plan, you should consider the following points:

- Look at possible escape routes via windows and doors. If you're in an apartment, there will be a fire escape plan posted in the hallway for the building already. Make sure you familiarize yourself with this, so you know what to do and you can follow this, in case of emergency. Your landlord should be able to provide you with a copy of this.

- If your fire alarm sounds, you should always leave the property as quickly and safely as possible. Stay low while in the building and call 911 once you've made your escape.

- Never use the elevator in the event of a fire.

- You should always escape via the nearest suitable exit. Go into every room in your apartment and consider how you can escape from each room.

- Doors keep fires back for several minutes, so you should close as many doors as possible between you and the fire.

- If smoke starts to appear in the room you're in or in the hallways (if you're trying to leave the building), stay low to the ground, as smoke rises.

- If you manage to get out, go to a specific meeting point (this is usually detailed in your fire plan), so people know you've made it out of the building.
- If you can't get out of the building, call 911, and stay low in your room with the door closed, until help arrives.
- If you're trapped in your room or apartment, try to make your location known to the firefighters, as they'll then make you a priority.
- Once you're outside and safe, the emergency services will let you know when it's safe to go back into the building.

If you don't have a fire evacuation plan from your landlord based on the building, you can still create one yourself using the points above. That way, you'll clearly know what to do in the event of a fire.

Safety first!

Furnishing Your Place

When you rent your first place, you'll want to make it a home. This means you'll want it in your style and some home comforts. Sometimes, you can rent a property that includes kitchen appliances and furniture. Apartment blocks sometimes have a laundry room, so there might be some things you don't need.

It's also worthwhile considering pre-owned furniture, as you can get some great deals. This really depends on your personal situation, what's included, and how much money you have available.

Before you buy anything, ensure you measure the dimensions of the rooms in your apartment, and also consider the access to the property. If your apartment is on the second floor or higher, it may limit your options. It's a good idea to draw a floor plan of your place, if possible.

Generally, the furniture you'll need for your first apartment could include:

- a sofa
- a side table
- a desk
- a dresser
- a two-person table and chairs
- a bed

If your apartment doesn't have certain kitchen appliances, you may need to buy those items too. You'll also need kitchenware, tableware, curtains, electronic items (such as a television), towels, bedsheets and blankets, pillows, and any other decorative items you feel you need. It's important that you only buy the things you consider essential items for now, as you'll have plenty of time to buy the non-essential items later.

The three most important items to consider buying first, in this particular order, are:

1. a bed (so you have somewhere to sleep)
2. a sofa (so you have somewhere to sit)
3. a desk (so you have somewhere to work or study)

If you are buying these items brand new from a store, it's a good idea to shop around and watch out for sales. You may be offered interest-free credit, so you won't have to pay the full amount for the items all at once; you pay for them over a series of months.

If it's interest-free, it means you are not charged interest for paying this way. For instance, if a bed costs $300 and you can pay for it on an interest-free agreement, by spreading the cost over six months, you'll be charged $50 per month, which totals $300. If you are paying interest on an item, you'll pay an extra charge on top of that, so you may pay $55 per month, which brings it to $330 for the bed in total. You should always ensure that you can afford to pay for this, as you will enter into a credit agreement, which is legally binding. If you do have the money to pay for items outright, this is sometimes the best thing to do.

Once you've bought the relevant furniture for your home, it's time to keep it clean.

Keeping the Apartment Clean

You should get into the habit of keeping your apartment clean, as much as possible. You should give it a thorough cleaning before you move in, ensuring you wash the paintwork, floors, walls, appliances, and any storage spaces. Windows and doors will also need cleaning, and you'll want to clean out your bathroom and your sinks.

If any of your rooms have carpet, they will need to be vacuumed. Doing this twice per week is usually fine, but if you live in a busy home that has regular visitors or a pet, you might choose to run the vacuum daily. To wash your carpets, you need a carpet cleaning machine, or you could do this with detergent and a scrubbing brush. You don't need to wash your carpets daily, and again, it depends on how grubby the carpet gets. Use your discretion on this one!

Wooden floors are usually swept with a broom and the floors are washed or polished, depending on the type of wood. You can buy floor cleaners suitable for the type of floor you have.

When you're cleaning your windows, you'll need glass cleaner and a cloth. It's a good idea to wipe in a circular motion to remove streaks. You can also do this when cleaning any mirrors inside the property. You should clean your windows on a monthly basis.

There are many surface cleaners that you can buy to wash work surfaces. Many of these can also be used in the bathroom, for your toilet, sinks, shower, and bath, but you may choose to use a harsher substance, such as something with bleach or a limescale remover for certain jobs. If you have some wooden furniture items or ornaments, you can use furniture polish with a duster to remove dust, rather than dirt. You should clean your surfaces and bathroom daily, if possible— your kitchen surfaces should be cleaned every time you cook or make a meal in the kitchen.

You can buy disinfectant cheaply that you simply mix with water to wash both surfaces and floors. It's also possible to make your own cleaners too. A one-to-one ratio of white vinegar and water is good for cleaning your windows, surfaces, and floors; however, you shouldn't use it on certain metals (such as stainless steel) and granite, as it can cause corrosion. You can also add a few drops of your favorite essential oil, to make it smell better, or even a squeeze of lemon and some herbs, such as rosemary.

A good cleaner to make for your stove includes four tablespoons of baking powder to four cups of warm water. This is also great for stainless steel and for removing odors too.

Now you know how to clean the home, let's talk about clutter.

How to Maintain a Decluttered Home—Top Five Tips

The more things you have, the more tidying you have to do. It's best to keep your home as clutter-free as possible. When we have a decluttered home, we can also attempt to declutter our minds.

- Be mindful of the things you buy, because it's easy to fill your home with things. Try to be a minimalist, and when it comes to spending, always play the waiting game, and consider if you want it or need it. Needs are a priority, but if you want it, you need to think about whether you really want it or if it is just a fleeting desire. You can wait a while before buying—there's no rush, and you should always challenge it by considering why you want it before you buy it.
- Have a place for everything. If you don't have a place for it, then you don't need it. Don't be afraid to purge and throw out or donate the things you don't want or need anymore. This may even make room for something new from time to time, but if you're going to buy something, make sure you have somewhere to store it.
- Get into the habit of tidying daily. Commit to tidying up so it becomes a daily habit, as this can help to ensure you have a clutter-free home. Schedule in some time each day to put things

away and clean up the clutter. Use a storage or laundry basket to collect any loose items, and then you can put them away as you walk through each room, tidying everything along the way. It's also good practice to make your bed each day and put your worn clothes straight in the laundry basket. You'll find it only takes you 10 minutes or less, most days.

- Give your kitchen a good cleaning daily. Declutter and wipe over the surfaces and stove after use. Make sure you also put everything away in its place in the kitchen. If you take out the milk, put it back in the refrigerator, for example.

- Keep your paperwork under control. You may find you have a lot of paperwork, such as your lease agreement, insurance documents, and bills. Find a folder or somewhere suitable to keep your paperwork in, and file it in a place where you can access it. When your mail arrives, put it in a collection tray, and once you've dealt with it, file it away or dispose of it. Many people are stepping away from paperwork, so if you are able to, try to scan your paperwork and store it electronically in the cloud or on a memory stick, if possible.

Thinking of Getting a Pet

It's important to cover one final topic because, in this chapter, we've focused on rental properties, and while some of this information is the same when you're buying a home, one thing that can be different in a rental property, is whether you're able to keep a pet.

If you're thinking of getting a pet, you should contact your landlord first and ask if this is possible. Some landlords don't allow pets, and sometimes this is written into your lease. It may be a strict rule that no pets are allowed, or maybe they are, with written consent, so that means you would have to write to your landlord and ask before you get a pet. If you don't, you could be in breach of your lease agreement, which could see you evicted from your home, and you could lose your deposit as a result. It's also possible that, if pets are allowed, you have to pay an extra amount each month with your rent and you need to consider if this is something you can afford or not.

In addition to this, it's important to consider just how much time and commitment it takes to own a pet, so there's a lot you need to think about first. You have to be able to care for your pet well, so if you get a dog and you're out at work all day, who's going to care for it?

Speaking of dogs, let's use them as an example.

Dogs need walking twice per day and feeding one to three times per day, depending on the dog. They also need access to pet care, as they require vaccinations and regular health check-ups. In many locations, you have to register as a dog owner, but rules vary, depending on where you live. Dogs can sometimes have accidents or develop medical conditions, so it's recommended that you have pet insurance too, so you aren't hit with unexpected bills that cost thousands of dollars.

The cost of the insurance will depend on the dog's type, age, any current health conditions, and where you live, and it's only valid if you keep up with its check-ups and vaccinations. It's good to shop around or visit comparison sites when you're looking for pet insurance.

You have to really consider if you can afford any pet—even rabbits, birds, and cats can end up costing you time and money, and insurance is recommended for them too. You also need to think about who can care for your pet when you're on vacation or if you are ill, as they're your sole responsibility. Fish are probably the least demanding of pets and can be quite therapeutic.

Don't forget; you have to clean up after your pet too. Cats have litter trays, and rabbits and birds have cages, which need to be cleaned out regularly. Dogs tend to use the outdoors for their toilet requirements; however, you still have to clean this up, otherwise you'll end up with an insect infestation. Cats, dogs, and rabbits need their nails clipped occasionally by professionals, and sometimes they need to be groomed too.

Anyone who doesn't take care of their pets properly can face criminal charges and have their animals removed. As well as speaking to your landlord, you should seriously consider whether or not you're ready to commit to maintaining a pet. Although it may seem like a good idea at the time, many people give up their pets as they discover they don't have the time, money, or patience to care for them properly.

Activity #2: Cleaning Checklist

It can be difficult to remember exactly what you need to clean when you first move into your home, especially if you haven't done a lot of chores or been involved in housework when you lived at home with your parents. Here is a list of cleaning tasks. Print it out or create your own list. Tick them off as you complete them. Not all of them will apply, but most of them will. You may even need to add something if I've missed it.

Every day you should:

- make your bed
- do the dishes
- take out the trash
- wipe over the bathroom sink, bath, shower, and toilet
- wipe down the kitchen surfaces and sink
- put dirty clothes in the laundry basket
- put clean clothes away in the closet or dresser
- wipe down tables
- do a quick tidy-up before bed, putting things in their place; books on the shelf, papers in the paper tray, etc.

Every week (or twice per week) you should:

- dust relevant wooden or plastic surfaces
- vacuum, sweep, and/or mop floors
- clean the mirrors
- change your bed sheets and wash the dirty sheets

- do the laundry
- give the bathroom a good, deep clean
- clean the kitchen appliances, inside and out
- go through your fresh food and throw out anything that's expired
- give the kitchen a deep clean.

Every month you should:

- dust fans and vents
- scrub your stove top and inside your stove
- vacuum upholstery
- clean out your indoor trash cans
- wipe down any cabinets in the kitchen
- clean your switches, television remotes, and doorknobs

Every three to six months, you may need to:

- wash your curtains, drapes, shades, or blinds
- vacuum the mattress on your bed
- clean any leather furnishings
- dust your lampshades and lighting
- polish your stainless steel
- clean and descale your iron, coffee maker, or kettle
- wipe down baseboards
- wash your windows, both inside and out
- wash cushions and any sofa coverings.

Feel free to add anything to your own list that I've missed. This is just to get you started.

Start on your daily list today and tick off as many items as possible. If you manage to complete every task on that part of the list, reward yourself!

We've started building good cleaning habits, but in the next chapter, we'll move onto building good money habits.

CHAPTER 3

Building Good Money Habits

Y ou probably feel like rolling your eyes at me as we move on and talk about money matters, but don't worry, this chapter will be quick and simple, as you'll learn the key things you need to learn, without feeling bogged down and overwhelmed.

There are six short sections in this chapter that cover budgeting, information on different bank accounts, savings, debt, your credit profile, and how to pay taxes.

By the end of this chapter, you'll be more confident when it comes to handling your money, which will allow you to work on good money habits that will last a lifetime.

Whether you want to talk about it or not, money is an important aspect of your life, and you should consider this:

Wealth is largely the result of habit.

–JOHN JACOB ASTOR

Let's start by talking about budgeting.

Budgeting

Budgeting is a really effective way to manage your money. It means that you keep track of what you have available each month and also allows you to see exactly what you spend. This is called tracking your finances.

- Calculate your available income. To budget, you need to know what your net income is. This means the money you have once your deductions have been made, along with any taxes you owe. Your retirement plan deductions and your health insurance can be deducted before you calculate your net income. Whatever is left after these deductions is your take-home pay, but to calculate your total income, you need to add this to any other income you receive (allowances, side hustles, for example), and this is basically what you have left to pay your bills and other expenses.

- Track your spending. Make a list of all the things you MUST pay every month and detail the amount you pay for each. This could include your rent; if you have a car, you need to detail your car expenses, such as insurance and gas; your utilities; your groceries; and any other financial commitments you have, such as credit cards, loans, your cell phone, and gym memberships.

- Generally, your total income should be more than you're spending. If you're aware of how much you spend and what you spend your money on, you can start to make cutbacks, if necessary. If you have money left over, that's ideal as really, you should be setting financial goals to help you save for the future, such as your retirement and being able to buy property.

- Compare your income and expenses to see how your finances are looking right now. A good guide for what you should spend and save is the 50/30/20 rule. 50% of your income should go toward the things you MUST pay each month. 30% should be used for your leisure activities, such as your gym membership, eating out, and other social activities. The final 20% of your income should be saved. We'll talk about your savings a little later in this chapter.

- Based on your comparison, set realistic goals. Some of your goals will be short-term, while others will be long-term. Some people want to pay off debts, save an emergency fund, and save a deposit for a home, or save for their summer holiday in the short term, but then they still want to save something for their retirement in the long term.

- Form a financial plan. Examine and prioritize your goals, and consider what you want to achieve. If you don't have enough money coming in, you may want to consider other ways to make money or you may choose to look at your spending and make cutbacks. Sometimes, we're paying for app subscriptions that we don't really need, so we can cancel them and save some money. Anything you can cut back on is a win! Redirect your money—if you can only follow a 70/10/20 finance plan for now, do it. You can always review your finances as your income increases.

Bank Accounts

There are different options when you open a bank account. Different banks may offer you different deals, which could be in your favor. Be sure to shop around to see what incentives are being offered.

Generally, when you're a young adult, you want either a checking account or a student account. Let's explore these:

- A checking account is your main bank account, and it means that you usually have a bank or debit card to use in shops or to withdraw money, so you don't have to carry all your cash around with you. Your bank keeps a record of your spending and withdrawals. You can also use this type of account to pay your bills and you can set up the payment to happen every month. That means your bills are paid automatically, so you don't have to think about it. All you have to do is ensure the money is in your account. There are three common types of payments:
  - Direct debits—regular payments, set up by the company you are paying (usually you need to inform the company you're paying if you wish to cancel, and the amount can be amended by the company only).
  - Standing orders—regular payments, set up by you (you can cancel or change the amount you pay anytime).
  - Direct recurring payments—this is usually a regular, agreed payment, charged to your debit card by the company you need to pay. Usually, this is when you use a subscription service, and they need to be canceled by

the company, if possible. However, you can contact your bank if there are any issues.

- Student accounts are very similar; they simply recognize that you are a student and, therefore, may not have as much money as someone who has a full-time job or career. Sometimes, students are offered different incentives to those with a regular checking account, so it's worth speaking to your bank if you are a student, to see what they can offer you.

To apply for a bank account, you simply head to the website. You click to apply for an account and complete the information on the application form. You then need to pass an identity and security check, and sometimes this means going in person to the bank with your identification. Finally, you activate your account when you put in some money.

You can sign up for your banking app with the relevant bank, which means you can view your transactions (what's come in and gone out of your account), what your balance is, and any bills that are due to be taken. You can also download your statement, and every month a bank statement will be available to you, showing your deposits and withdrawals for the previous month. This can be received online, or it can be a paper-based statement sent to you in the mail.

You should check your bank statement to ensure everything is as it should be. When you see the word 'debit,' it means the amount deducted or taken from your account, but if you see the word 'credit,' it's the amount added to your account. You should always review all the transactions (incoming and outgoing) and ensure they're familiar to you. Look for any charges you don't recognize or anything suspicious, and if you find anything suspicious, call your bank and inform them right away, as you need to protect yourself from fraud. Make sure you always cancel monthly payments that are no longer in use, as you don't want money to be taken unexpectedly. You can usually do this easily via your mobile app or internet banking.

Another type of bank account you may see advertised by your bank, is a savings account.

Savings

A savings account is a way to save some of your money, and there are many different types of savings accounts. You basically put money in a savings account that you don't want to spend, so you separate it from the rest of your money. Usually, you are paid a better interest rate on your savings than on a checking account. The more you save, the more interest you receive. Any interest you receive is taxable income, so when you're choosing a savings account, always read the terms and conditions to look out for charges and fees.

If you want to save for your first home, a car, or for a vacation, a savings account will separate your money and keep it until you decide to withdraw it. If you want to access your money quickly, be sure to check the terms of your savings account. Easy access accounts will offer you instant access to your money, whereas a fixed-term savings account means you need to save over a specified period of time, so if you withdraw before the agreed-upon time, there will be a charge. A regular savings account usually doesn't offer a high interest rate, and if you're serious about saving over a number of years, there are other savings and investment accounts that may suit you better.

Emergency Funds

An emergency fund is your security as an adult. It's an amount (that you decide) that you save and keep to one side for unexpected events and emergencies. Let's say you have a car, and it breaks down, and you need to fix it; you can then use your emergency fund to pay for that. It's a good idea to set a financial goal for your emergency fund. It's recommended that you have at least six months of your salary saved, so if you lost your job, you could cover your expenses for six months. Start small, and aim for a couple of hundred dollars, and then reassess when you've achieved your goals.

Investing

If you save a lump sum and are able to commit to investing, it can certainly be worthwhile. While savings are good in the short term, investing is a long-term commitment.

There are four main types of investments:

1. Cash assets—they are short-term investments of 90 days or less. They offer a low return on your investment and are low risk and sometimes used while a person is waiting for a better long-term investment opportunity.
2. Growth assets—they are medium to high-risk investments that rely on the market and economy. They can deliver high returns, but you must be able to commit to investment for at least five years.

3. Commodity assets—they are investments in basic goods, like wheat, for instance. Although they are low-cost, such a market can be unpredictable. The benefits are that it diversifies your portfolio of investments.

4. Defensive assets—they are low to medium-risk but require your investment for at least two years. They are a stable investment; however, returns are often low.

Before you invest, make sure you have your emergency fund first, and then try to keep at least $1,000 on top of that, for safety. If you want to invest, the more money you have the better, but it must be money that you can do without for at least five years. Some investments allow you to invest from as little as $10, but for some investment types, you're looking at $500–1,000 or more, or even between $5,000–$10,000. Basically, if you're wanting to invest, you can do this at any time; however, if you have a sum of money, you would be best speaking to a certified financial advisor to find out which investments will serve you best. Financial goals and needs are different for everyone, and a financial advisor can help you come up with the best financial plan for you.

Retirement Plans

Many young adults don't consider their retirement, because it seems so far away; however, you should plan for your retirement as early as you possibly can. The cost of living is rising, so you have to allow for this when you're planning for your retirement, and the earlier you start to contribute, the less you have to worry about it later. Having a retirement plan in place is good practice, as it helps you get used to paying into your retirement earlier—it's a good money habit.

When planning for your retirement, you need to:

- Work out how much you'll need. The age of retirement is rising, and nobody knows exactly how long they'll live, so it means you should look at national averages. For example, look at what age you want to retire and the life expectancy average for your gender. You also need to allow for inflation and consider how much this will have risen by the time you retire, and then increase it for every year of your retirement.

- Choosing the right retirement plan for you. Sometimes, it's difficult to decide which would be the best option for you, so speaking to a reputable financial advisor who knows all about retirement plans is important:

    o Some people simply choose to save and invest, often in property or real estate, or in the stock market.

    o Others choose annuities, which is a type of insurance to help you keep money aside for your retirement. When you retire, you pay yourself an income. You make payments over time, or in a lump sum, and there are three common types:

        ▪ Fixed annuities—when you are provided a fixed income over your lifetime or for an agreed number of years.

- Fixed indexed annuities—this ties you into the stock index, but if it doesn't perform well, your annuity will still hold its value.
- Variable annuities—this gives you plenty of opportunities to grow your money; however, there is a higher risk. Your payout depends on how well your investments into stocks and bonds perform.
  - Income stream retirement—this is when you create several income streams that you can use on your retirement. Let's say you bought property, and now have a rental revenue to give you an income every month, but you also own the property and have this as collateral.

Some people choose to have a phased retirement or head into a second career when they've hit retirement age, as they feel they want to slow down, but also bring in an income. It's definitely worth considering your retirement, and once you have a full-time income, you should contact a reputable financial advisor to make a retirement plan—it's never too early!

Debts

Your debts are basically the money you owe to financial companies, and they are charging you interest (a fee) over the period you owe them money. If you owe money on loans, credit cards, store cards, or you have an overdraft, or something else that means you are paying interest and signed an agreement, these are your debts.

You should always pay your debts off first before you begin saving, because your debts are a priority. The interest financial companies are charging you for your debts will be more than the interest you will earn on savings, so it's important to get them under control as soon as possible.

If you have debts, total up the amount you owe. Create some financial goals to pay off your debts—how much can you afford to pay each month? When it comes to the 50/30/20 financial rule we reviewed, try 50/50 if you can afford it, and use 50% of your income for your expenses and the other 50% of your income to pay off your debts (or as much as you can, as debts should come before your non-essential wants and leisure, and savings).

Try to write down a plan of action based on your goals, when tackling your debts. Prioritize your debts, paying off the most expensive first. Start with the debt that charges you the most interest and pay this one off first to reduce the amount of interest you're paying. If you need help with your debts, don't be afraid to speak to a certified financial advisor.

Your Credit Profile

All adults have a credit file or profile. This includes personal financial data stored about you that gives financial institutions an idea of whether you're a financial risk, if they allow you to borrow money. From this information, a credit score is calculated, and the higher your score, the more likely you are to be able to get credit. If you have a credit card, but have been sensible with this, and have paid it back, your score will improve; however, if you miss a payment or spend irresponsibly, your score will be lowered. Your creditors will also be able to decide how much they can lend you, based on your income, current financial commitments, and your credit score.

Paying Your Taxes

Although the thresholds change every year, most people in America, who are US citizens, permanent residents, and who work in the US, must file their taxes if they earn above a certain amount. Currently, everyone who earns more than $12,950 has to file their tax return with the IRS by April of every year.

You can file on paper; however, it's easier to file your taxes online, as they are processed much faster. Filing your return helps you to avoid interest and penalties, provides an accurate picture of your income, protects your credit, and ensures you can apply for financial aid, if applicable. This can also give you peace of mind and help you build your social security benefit, if necessary. In some cases, you could get money back from your taxes too, so it's certainly worthwhile. To file your return, you should head over to www.irs.gov where you can find out more information and file for free. If you need help with your return, there are websites and specialist tax advisors out there who can help you, or you could speak to parents or family members too.

Activity #3: Your Budget

1. Create a budget, by listing your incoming money each month, and listing your payments. Copy the template below.
2. Work out how much you can save, but remember, if you have any debt, you should pay this off first.

Date	Description	Incoming Amount	Spending Amount
	Payment from work	*$3000.00*	
	Rent payment		*$700.00*
	Internet charges		*$50.00*
	Cell phone charges		*$90.00*
	Savings account		*$300.00*

	TOTAL	*$3000.00*	*$1140.00*

1. Based on this information, create three long- or short-term financial goals.
2. Consider how much you can save each month.

Now that you're getting into good money habits, it's time to move on and talk about the skills you need to develop when you're adulting. Let's talk about personal growth!

CHAPTER 4

Essential Day-to-Day Skills

Where are my clean clothes?
What's for dinner?

Do these questions sound familiar? Of course they do. They're questions you've asked your parents a thousand times. But you can't ask these questions when you no longer live with them. These are things you're going to be responsible for yourself as an adult, and this can be a learning curve.

> *Every day of your life is another lesson. If you learn the lesson well and apply it, whether positive or negative, you determine what happens in your tomorrow.*
>
> –DAVID KOFI AWUSI

The skills you're about to learn in this chapter will help you adult better, while also aiding your personal growth. Again, we've made this as focused as possible, because we want to make adulting as easy as possible for you. That's why we're going to talk about being organized, studying skills, skills around the house, and cooking on a budget.

If you can master the skills in these four categories, adulting will be a breeze for you!

Let's talk about being organized first, because it's the foundation of everything when you're an adult.

Being Organized

What if I told you that you're already organized?

You've probably been told that you need to be more organized a million times, and yet, nobody really tells us how to develop that skill. You've already been working on your organization skills in the first three chapters of the book, so you're already ahead—you've got an A grade for that!

When we talked about goal-setting, starting a side hustle, skills for your career, brain-dumping or listing ideas, scheduling viewings for apartments, cleaning and decluttering your home, budgeting, when you complete your school assignments, your fire safety plan, and organizing your finances—they all require you to use your skills of organization. We just need to take those skills (which you already have), develop them, and apply them to other areas of your life.

It's that simple!

When we're talking about you being organized, we need to focus on your schedule. Now, everyone's schedule is different, and that's okay. You're not going to be told what your schedule is, you're going to figure it out and ensure you're doing what works best for you.

When you're organizing your schedule, you need to think about the things you MUST do every day:

- Sleep—what time should you go to bed and how much sleep do you need?
- Wake up—what time do you have to wake up, in order to get to school or work, or other commitments each day?
- Wash, shower, and dress—when will you get these things done?
- Go to school—what time does school start?
- Go to work—what time do you need to be at work?
- Eat (mealtimes)—what time is breakfast, lunch, and dinner? If you're making your own dinner, remember to allow time for this in your schedule too.
- Nonnegotiables—what are the other things that you have to do? This could be fitness classes, watching your favorite TV shows, time reading your book, and socializing with friends, for example.

They are the things you're going to input into your schedule first, and everything else you have to do will fit around this. Ask yourself:

- When will I study?
- When will I do my laundry?
- When will I clean my apartment?
- What day is the garbage disposal in my area?
- What day will I take care of the garden?
- When will I have time for myself?

Some adults try to cost-save when it comes to food, so they cook in bulk, and store food for the week in the refrigerator or freezer. They also take their lunch to work or school to save money, so they don't have to purchase it. If you do any of these things, remember to create time in your schedule to prepare your meals.

You're probably wondering why it's so important to be organized, but there are many benefits. First, it reduces stress levels, because you know what to do and when to do it, in a similar way you do when goal setting. You also know where your things are, and organization strengthens your ability to keep your place clean and tidy, which promotes good health. It allows you time to focus on the things that really matter, for instance, you'll be able to focus on getting good sleep, eating healthier, studying well, and it's also believed to increase your productivity at work. Organization also improves the relationships in your life, because you'll be able to focus on them and you'll generally be happier, because of the type of lifestyle you have.

Think

Are there any aspects of your life that you'd like to improve, in relation to your organizational skills?

Small, impactful changes can make a big difference!

Study Skills for Your Success

Having time to study, even if it's self-study for personal growth purposes, can be a pivotal aspect of your life. Here are 10 top tips to ensure your studying is a success:

1. Ensure you've designated time in your schedule to study and, if possible, make this early in the morning, as many studies suggest this is when we're most productive. According to Stych (2019) in BizJournals.com, 44% of people say they're more productive in the early morning, while 31% of people say they're more productive late morning.

2. Keep a clear and organized workspace to study in, and ensure you have everything you need close by, such as your laptop, a pen, highlighters, books, papers, a headset, your notebook, a stapler, a lamp, and anything else you feel is essential to your studies.

3. Read through your syllabus well to ensure you understand your topic and have plenty of time to study all relevant subtopics.

4. Create a weekly or daily to-do list and turn your list into goals. Set yourself clear goals for the week ahead, and then draw out what you need to do each day. This way, you'll know what you want to achieve in each study session.

5. Schedule plenty of breaks, even if it's just a walk to the kitchen to make refreshments or have a snack.

6. Don't feel like you have to stay at your desk—move around if you can. You may want to stand up or even walk around while

you read a book or paper. Moving around can really help with motivation.

7. Be creative with your studying—use pens, highlighters, diagrams, and sticky notes to make your notes visually appealing. This will help you organize your notes and key facts, points, or opinions, which will mean you can access your information easily. This will increase your productivity.

8. Reward yourself for your achievements throughout your study sessions.

9. Schedule in some "me" time. You need "me" time; however, you don't want this to eat into your study time, so schedule it when you think it works well.

10. Have a study buddy or study group, whom you can be in contact with to keep you motivated. You can do this online or on your cell phone, and if you get stuck, your buddies may be able to help you.

Skills Around the House

We've already talked about cleaning your home, so you already have some skills to use around the house. We've also given food and mealtimes their own section (the next chapter), so in this section, we're going to talk about laundry, ironing, and storing your clothes.

Laundry

When we do laundry, we split our clothes up in a particular way. There are five ways to do this, and generally, this is based on color.

1. Any laundry that is completely white must be washed together.
2. Light-colored clothing should be washed together. This could be striped whites, pastel shades, etc.
3. Dark-colored clothing should be put together, such as blacks, browns, and dark blues.
4. Bright clothing should also be separate, and this includes oranges, reds, and yellows.
5. Delicates—these could be your fine linens, some underwear, silk or satin fabrics, and other synthetics that go together.

Good news! Your clothing has labels inside that tell you how to best wash it. Some clothing should be handwashed or dry-cleaned, so ensure you read the labels carefully on each of your garments and take anything with special requirements to a professional.

Try to keep each of your clothing piles small, so they are washed well— your machine should never be more than ¾ full, and overloading can break the machine. Be aware that sometimes your bright clothes will need to be washed alone for the first few washes, as their colors may run into other laundry, which will distort the color.

If your clothing has a stain on it, you may need to use a stain-remover treatment before washing. It's also important to remember that not all clothes can be dried in a dryer, either. Some items may need hanging up or placing on an indoor or outdoor airer, to dry naturally.

To dry clothes in a dryer, be sure it is safe to do so on the label and check the guidance for your items. Put the clothes in the machine and close the door. Select either a cool or high temperature setting (depending on the garments you're drying). Turn the dial and select a time. It's best if you don't dry your items for too long, as it can ruin the items, make them extremely wrinkled, and make the fabric stiff. When you first start drying your clothes, set them for 30 minutes, and then check them every 10–20 minutes after this—they should feel dry, yet soft.

It's up to you to choose what detergent you use on your laundry, as we all have our preferences. Tide Purclean is described as being the best laundry detergent, as it's eco-friendly, yet Persil ProClean Sensitive Skin is said to work best for those who have sensitive skin or allergies. There are so many excellent brands that are cost-effective and have additional in-wash scents to make your laundry smell amazing, so the choice is yours.

Ironing and Iron Care

Once your clothing is dry, you can iron it, if needed. There are certain fabrics that you can't iron, so please read the label first. There will be ironing guidelines within your garment, and your iron also comes with instructions, so make sure you select the right temperature, depending on the garment. Generally, there is a low temperature for acrylics and nylon, a medium temperature for silk, satin, wool, and polyester, and a high temperature setting for denim, linen, and cotton. If the iron is too cold, it won't get wrinkles out of your garments, and if it's too hot, it will burn your garments, and sometimes, it sticks to it and creates a hole.

To iron a garment:

- Set up the ironing board.

- Turn your garment inside-out.

- Smooth your garment or part of your garment over the board (one pant leg, for instance).

- Run the iron over your garment, moving the hot iron up and down and keeping it as tight as possible.

- Fold up your clothing item and place it somewhere (to be put away later).

- You don't need to iron your underwear, socks, or hats.

Iron Care

You need to take care of your iron, so when you've finished with it, unplug it and wait for it to cool down. Drain the iron by tipping it forward over the sink, allowing the unused water to pour out. Use a damp cloth to rub the metal plate until it's clean, and then dry it with a cloth. Sometimes, an iron develops limescale and needs to be descaled. You can buy a descaler from the store. If you need to descale your iron, be sure to read the instructions on the box.

Tidying Away Your Clothes

Once you've ironed your clothes, it's time to put them away. Your shirts, blouses, dresses and suits should be hung in your closet. But your jeans and tops can be stored in your dresser or on suitable shelves inside your closet.

Cooking on a Budget

For many people, the rising cost of living means that we're looking to cut costs, so we're often on a budget when it comes to food and cooking.

There are some things you can do to maximize your budget when cooking, yet you can still eat healthy meals, and you can still eat well. I've got some great tips just for you!

- Meal plan—if you're cooking on a budget, you should make a weekly meal plan. This means you're less likely to spend extra cash in the grocery store or buy fast food. Planning meals can also help to reduce food waste, so you're doing your part for the environment.

- Use your leftovers—if you can, try to use your leftovers from your evening meal. If you take lunch to work or school, store your leftovers in the refrigerator and take them with you the next day.

- Create your grocery list—when you go to the store, make sure you've written a grocery list. You should use your meal plan to help you form this, to ensure you buy the right ingredients and can cook the meals on your meal plan.

- Buy in bulk—you can often save money if you buy in larger quantities. While it can be expensive on the day you make the purchase, you'll save money the next few times you buy groceries. Buying staples, such as pasta and rice, is often cheaper if you bulk-buy, and they can make several nutritious meals.

- Batch cook—spend a weekend day cooking in batches. Cooking large amounts of food can work out cheaper, especially if you use lentils or vegetables to bulk out your meals. You can then separate this into portions, put the portions in the fridge or freezer, and serve as necessary.

When storing your food, perishable items, like dairy and meat, need to be in the refrigerator. Food labels specify how the items should be stored. Items are generally frozen if we want to store them for a long period of time. You should check that the items are suitable for freezing first, and when you want to use them, ensure they thaw thoroughly (unless you've bought it frozen and the label specifies you can "cook from frozen").

Other items, such as dried goods, should usually be stored in a cool, dark place. Your pantry is a great place to store such items, including canned goods and jars. Just be aware that, sometimes once these goods are opened, they may need to be stored differently (in the refrigerator, in a suitable container), so always read the label.

Some great quick and easy items that you can cook and then freeze for later include:

- chili con carne
- soups (of your choice—meat or vegetable)
- chicken casserole
- spaghetti sauce
- pan pizza
- meatloaf (vegetarian option also possible)
- beef or vegetable pies

You can find so many recipes on the internet for quick and easy meals that can be frozen for later. You won't be disappointed. Choose some of these items and make a list of the ingredients you need—don't forget to add them to your grocery list.

To fully equip your kitchen for cooking, you need to make sure you have:

- A kitchen knife set—you need a set of small to large knives, that are used for different purposes (cutting meat, cutting and peeling vegetables, a bread knife).
- Pots and pans—you will need a variety of pans suitable for cooking.
- Cutting boards—you need boards to cut items on, so your knives don't damage your kitchen surfaces and to avoid contamination.
- Utensils—such as wooden spoons, ladles, tongs, and spatulas.

Activity #4: Create a Meal Plan and Shopping List

- Use the template below to form a meal plan for a week. Before you begin, imagine you're on a budget—what budget will you set?
- Try to create some budget meals, using pasta, potatoes, and rice. If you eat meat, you could also try to have at least one meat-free day during the week.
- Try not to waste food—how can you use up your leftovers? Will one of the meals you make feed you more than once?

	Breakfast	Lunch	Dinner	Snacks and Drinks
Monday				
Tuesday				
Wednesday				
Thursday				
Friday				
Saturday				
Sunday				

- Once you've planned your meals for the week, produce a grocery list that includes all the ingredients you need.
- Use the internet to price up your grocery list and see how much you've spent.
- Is this within your budget? Is there any way you could reduce the cost of your groceries this week, or next week, based on the food you have?

When you're bulk-buying groceries, it's useful if you have a car to transport your goods from the store to your home. When you own a car, there's much more to it, as you have to pay for its maintenance too. Let's talk about buying your first car and how you can take care of it in the next chapter.

CHAPTER 5

Buying Your First Car and Taking Care of It

O wning your own car sounds like a dream, *right*? You can't wait for the day when you can hop in your car and drive across the state. Or head to your local Taco Bell drive-in, for a late-night snack.

If you have a car, you can do those things. But there's so much more involved when you own your first car. What does it really mean and how do you know if you can even afford it?

In this chapter, we're going to talk about buying a car. We'll discuss the benefits of having a car and consider how this can help your career. By the end of the chapter, you'll be "in the know" when it comes to the various expenses involved with owning a car, and we'll talk about making the purchase and what you need to look out for, especially if you're buying a used car. We'll also touch on basic maintenance.

Having a car is awesome, but as a young adult, you need to know the facts and what to expect. When it's time for you to buy your first car, you've got this!

The Benefits of Owning a Car

Of course, there are many benefits of owning a car, so we can't forget that. It's an exciting time, and you should be excited about it. It's a huge deal for you! Cars are associated with freedom, so owning one means you can essentially go wherever you want, whenever you want. You don't have to wait for a cab, an Uber, or a bus, which means you save time, and if the weather is stormy or too hot, you don't have to be uncomfortable as you wait for your transport.

Taking the Plunge and Buying a Car

If you want a car, you need to consider if you're going to lease a car or buy one. If you want to own your own car, you then have to decide if you're going to buy a brand-new car from a dealership, or if you're buying a pre-owned car.

Buying a car from a dealership often comes with a warranty, which means the dealership will fix it (within reason), if something goes wrong. Cars that are brand new cost a lot more money. You can buy a car on credit; however, you need to have a good credit score, in order to qualify.

If you buy a second-hand, or pre-owned car, there are risks involved, as sometimes they are not in the best condition, they may need several repairs, and the car can cost more to maintain because it's older.

When you're buying a car, you should:

- Decide if you want an electric car, or a car that takes gas or fuel.

- Decide if you want to buy a new or used car.
- Look at several cars and consider prices.
- Ask to take it for a test drive—don't be afraid to ask questions if there are any strange noises or other concerns.
- Perform additional checks, such as:
    - checking the vehicle documents
    - checking the vehicle mileage
    - considering how many previous owners the vehicle has had
    - reviewing the vehicle history (check the Carfax report, and ensure you have information on services and repairs)
    - arranging an independent inspection—don't skip on this step, it's vital. If the seller refuses this, there could be something seriously wrong with the vehicle.
- Negotiate the price—you have the right to negotiate. You may get perks and extras, or even a discount, especially if you're buying a used car.
- Think about how you want to pay for your car. Will you be buying it outright? Will you be looking for an auto loan? Will you be putting down a big deposit?
- Find out if taxes are included in the sales price or if you need to file them.
- Sign your contract to confirm you're buying the vehicle.
- Obtain the title certificate or certificate of ownership if the car has been registered previously. If the vehicle is brand new, the

dealer will provide you with a statement of origin. Do not buy a car if you cannot be provided with either of these.

- Register the vehicle with the relevant DMV—sometimes, the car dealer can help you with this. To do this, you will need registration forms, your address, your driving license, your vehicle contract or purchase agreement, and your vehicle title certificate. You will also need to show car insurance proof or automobile liability insurance in some states, so let's talk about that next. Registration can take a few weeks.
- You may need to change the license plates for your vehicle, but this depends on your location. You'll be informed of the rules in your area by your dealer or the DMV.

Understanding Auto Insurance

To insure your car, you need to provide your driver's license. It's also a good idea to use a trustworthy broker to help you arrange your insurance, as this can be costly.

Some states require that you have auto insurance before you can start driving your car, or you could be fined or even face jail time. In most states, you must have basic liability insurance, which insures a person for bodily liability and covers the damage of their property. Each state has its own minimum requirements when it comes to auto insurance.

There are three main types of car insurance:

- Liability insurance—this covers the other driver's bodily injuries, and their property, if you're at fault during an accident.

- Collision insurance—this is for collisions with stationary objects or car accidents.
- Comprehensive coverage—this protects your vehicle from nondriving accidents, such as acts of nature or theft.

You will be responsible for the financial risks involved, so it's recommended that you get comprehensive and collision coverage, so you don't end up paying out of pocket. It's recommended that you speak to a broker, to ensure you're getting a policy that meets your needs and the requirement of the state you live in.

Taking Care of Your Car

Owning a car is expensive, and in addition to everything we've already discussed, you still need to be able to pay for gas, routine maintenance, repairs, parking costs, and any tickets you incur. Some people also opt for breakdown coverage, in case their car breaks down when they're traveling, as callouts are expensive.

It's recommended that your car is serviced at least once per year, or every 12,000 miles. Car services can cost between $150–250, but other car maintenance is also recommended. For example, your brake-pad replacement can cost $115–300, depending on your vehicle type and model. Tire rotation is another recommendation that can cost up to $100.

Before a long journey, you should carry out basic checks on your car. For example, you should top up windshield-wiper fluid and check your wipers to ensure they're in good working condition. You should also check your headlights, blinkers, brake lights, and parking lights to ensure they're all working well.

It's a good idea to check the oil every few weeks or before a long road trip. To do this, you need to lift the hood and pull out the dipstick to ensure it is above the minimum level. Your oil should be fully changed every three to six months, depending on how many miles you drive. This is usually done as part of a full service. It's important to note that some of the checks detailed here are only relevant to nonelectric cars.

You should check the coolant level in your vehicle too, as this can also lead to engine problems if it is too low. Refer to your car manual, as this will tell you how to find this.

Checking your tire pressure depends on what size tires you have and their type. It usually tells you in your manual or on the tire itself, detailed as the PSI level. Newer cars will usually alert you if your tire pressure is low. You should stop if the light comes on to alert you of this. If you want to know what your tire pressure is, take your car to a tire machine, remove the valve stem cap, and attach the pump. This will tell you what your tire pressure is at now, and then you can top it off, if need be. You should also check the tire treads to check if your tires need rotating or replacing.

To change a tire, ensure you pull your car safely off the road. You will need your car's manual, a wrench and wheel nut lock, a jack, and a wheel chock to keep the car from moving or rolling. Having a light can be helpful too.

Make sure everyone is out of the vehicle, apply the emergency brake, and take out the spare tire. Place the chocks behind the wheels of the car—the opposite tire to the one you're changing. Chock the other wheels too. Loosen the wheel nuts now, turning the wrench anti-clockwise—you need to jack the car up before you remove the tire completely.

Make sure you consult your vehicle manual frequently, as it will provide you with exact details of what to do. All vehicles have specific jacking points, so you'll need to know this before you jack the car. When jacking the vehicle, do this slowly until it's a few inches off the ground.

You can now fully remove the wheel nuts, and then you should pull the tire towards you until it releases. Roll it away and place it on the ground. Slide the spare tire onto the bolts and in line with the wheel nut slots, and then add the wheel nuts and tighten them by hand. Now you can bring the car back down to the ground fully. Make sure you check the nuts to ensure they're as tight as possible. You now need to check the tire pressure on your spare tire, so if you have a tire inflator, use it, or take your car to the nearest gas station. Pump the tire to the right pressure.

Don't forget to take your old tire with you! Sometimes, punctures can be repaired, so take it to the garage and find out if you need a new tire or if they can repair it for you. Your spare tire should only be used for emergencies, so you need to replace this as soon as possible.

Activity #5: Running a Basic Car Insurance Quote

For this activity, you need your laptop or personal computer, as you should head over to a car insurance comparison site and get a car insurance quote.

Use the details for the car of a person you know, such as your parents' car. Remember, you're not signing up for insurance, you're simply getting a free quote.

Run through the questions and answer them carefully, to the best of your ability. There will be lots of questions, options, and added extras to consider but running through this is good practice. While it's okay not to know everything, being able to get a free quote is extremely useful and it will give you an idea of how much a car will cost you. It shouldn't take you any longer than 15 minutes, so give it a try. In the next chapter, we'll move on from cars and start talking about your adult career.

CHAPTER 6

Your Work Life

W hat career excites you? What job do you dream of?
Whatever it is, it's up to you to make that dream come true.
You can have the career you want, but getting there is
sometimes a longer journey than you first anticipate. But that's okay,
because you're in charge of your own destiny.

If opportunity doesn't knock, build a door.

–MILTON BERLE

Some young adults have been working throughout their teens, but for
others, getting their first job is an exciting, yet slightly scary time. In
this chapter, we're going to focus on your first adult job, as you begin
your career.

The process of finding, applying, being interviewed, and being
recruited can be challenging, so the aim of this chapter is to make the
whole process as clear and as simple for you as possible. We're also
going to talk beyond recruitment, as we focus on excelling at work and
the soft skills you can develop as you strive toward a promotion.

We'll begin by focusing on getting your first adult job, and by the time this chapter is over, you'll be ready to blow away prospective employers.

What You Need to Know About Getting Your First Job

When you're ready to get your first adult job, you have to be willing to put the effort in and search. It can take time, so the most important thing is that you are patient.

The best way to find a job is to get online and search job websites. Search for specific jobs or career opportunities within a set distance of your home. Some businesses also place advertisement posters in their windows or details on their website, which they also share on their social media pages. If you have a specific career or company in mind, you can check out their job vacancies directly that way.

A job advertisement includes:

- The job title—so you know what job you're applying for.
- Salary details—so you know how much money you can expect to be paid.
- Location—so you know where you will work from, and if there is flexibility for remote working options available.
- Information about the business—usually the business briefly introduces itself in a few short sentences.
- Roles and responsibilities—which describe what's expected of you, if you are hired for this role.
- Key requirements—details of the type of person they need for the role, based on their qualifications, experience, and skills.

- How to apply for the role—the advertisement will usually provide you with details of how to apply for the job.

You then have to apply for the job, with all these things in mind. It's up to you to show the prospective employer how you will manage the key requirements of the role, and reflect on any experience that makes you capable of the roles and responsibilities.

When you're applying for a job, you need to create an irresistible application that employers just can't ignore.

Your Irresistible Application

There are several application methods to consider, and usually, the advertisement details which method you should choose:

- Resume—A resume is sometimes referred to as a CV. You should be as accurate and honest as possible on your resume, and in the document, you should include:

    o Your name, cell phone number, and email address.

    o A profile or summary, introducing yourself within a maximum of three sentences.

    o Your key skills and qualities (this can be tweaked to match the role you're applying for).

    o Education—schools, colleges, and qualifications, including dates of attendance.

    o Prior experience—any voluntary positions or jobs you've had that are relevant to the role.

- o Additional skills you've learned, such as soft skills, like time management, computer skills, communication skills, and research skills, etc.
- o Hobbies and interests—this gives a prospective employer an idea of the type of person you are.

- Portfolio—a portfolio includes samples of your work that are relevant to the role you're applying for. For example, a writer or artist may be asked to provide samples of their work, so prospective employers can see their skills and style.

- Cover letter—this is a letter that usually accompanies a resume, portfolio, or application, and it expresses your interest in the job you're applying for. This is written as a formal letter, but it's also your opportunity to explain why you are the perfect candidate for the role in question. When you write this, you should tell them how you match the key skills and qualities listed for the role.

- Application form—sometimes, an employer wants to know specific things, so rather than sending in a portfolio or resume, they want you to complete their company application form. You will be expected to complete the form, which will ask you for similar information that you usually include on your resume.

To ensure your application is irresistible, you should:

- Tailor your application to match the job description, and highlight how you meet the key requirements and skills for the role.

- Get to the point—they want to be able to assess your suitability for the role as quickly as possible, so get straight to the point.
- Use examples to give context to your skills.
- Highlight your successes—you need to be honest, but demonstrate knowledge of your strengths. You need to stand out from the crowd, so don't be shy to boast a little bit.
- Not down-play your soft skills. They are extremely important, and they are skills you can transfer into most jobs, like being able to work alone or in a team or organization skills. Do you have any other unique skills?
- Keep it short and sweet. A company can receive hundreds of applications for each job they advertise, and they don't have time to read larger documents. Put the most valuable information first, and give them a reason to read on.

An employer spends around eight seconds reviewing a resume. More than 80% of resumes don't even get moved on to the next step! If you don't want them to stop, you need to provide them with the key information they need, immediately. They'll only spend more time reading if they think your resume is worth it (Fennell, 2022).

Interview Skills

When you're invited to an interview, it's your chance to stand out and shine. It's important to spend time preparing for the interview, because it helps you feel more confident, and this will come across in your interview.

To set yourself up for success, you should prepare for your interview by:

- Researching the organization—take a look at the company website and look at their *About* section. This will give you the opportunity to find out what your employer is all about. Look at the products/services they offer, and read their goals, values, and mission statement. Learn as much as you can, so you can align your answers to the interview questions.

- Preparing to answer questions—it's important to practice answering interview questions, as this prevents you from feeling put on the spot during your interview and it also shows that you're taking your interview seriously. Although you won't know exactly what the interviewer will ask, you can look up some common interview questions. You should also read the job description, so you can come up with examples to use when answering the questions. Sometimes, you're asked to provide examples with your answers. If you have a friend or family member who is willing, you should use roleplay to practice being interviewed.

- Staying calm—before the interview, you may start to feel anxious or nervous, and this is normal. However, you must get it under control. Use breathing techniques or meditation to calm down and refocus your mind. A good breathing exercise is to breathe in for the count of four, hold your breath for four, and then breathe out for five. Breathing out for longer than you breathe in is said to calm you down. Concentrate on the breathing! We'll address relaxation methods and meditation in Chapter 8.

- Dressing for the occasion—you should show up for your interview looking professional. This means you need to be clean, well-groomed, and dressed in professional attire. If you're not sure exactly how professional, simply revisit the company website and consider the type of image they give off— this will give you a clue. Get your clothes ready the evening before to ensure nothing goes wrong on the day.

When you're in the interview itself:

- Make a good first impression—be polite, smile, and introduce yourself. Also, make sure you arrive on time.
- Listen carefully to the questions and make sure you answer the questions asked. You've done some preparation, but if you're unsure what the question means, don't be afraid to ask—it shows initiative.
- You should think of one or two questions to ask as well. You need to make sure that the organization you work for is the right company for you too, so ask them what they think is the biggest challenge in this role, what the company values the most, or something similar.
- Remember that an interview is a formal situation, so get your tone right, speak clearly, avoid using slang, and try to speak in a similar tone to the person interviewing you—but still be yourself. Use open and approachable body language, maintain eye contact, and smile!

After the interview, you can follow up with the company by sending them a thank you email. You then wait to hear if you are offered the job or not, and while it can be upsetting not to get the job, just remember it's a learning curve. Ask for feedback, if possible, on how you can improve. However, companies can't always provide this, due to the number of interviews they conduct, so don't worry if not. Assess the situation yourself and think about what you could do differently next time. Only one person gets the job out of several hundred applicants and many interviews, so you have to develop your resilience. Don't take it personally—it just wasn't meant to be and it's time to move on!

How to Excel at Work

It's important to make a good impression and excel at work, and there are certain things you can do to help you get a promotion faster. Let's explore some of these things.

Improve Your Communication Skills

Communication skills are important in everything you do at work and in life. If you develop these skills, you'll find it helps you to excel at work. Communication basically means the words we use to convey a message or information, so this could be oral or spoken communication, or it could also be written communication, which includes emails, reports or letters, for example. Your communication should be clear, concise, to the point, and it should be relevant. For example, if you have to present information to a group, you might use a written slide, but you would also present your ideas by talking through key points and answering questions. Working on your ability to present information well is an excellent way to excel in your job, as this is often a key role of a manager or leader.

Communication is not always about you directly communicating with others; it can also be in reference to how others communicate with you and how you respond. You should also work on your listening skills by listening carefully to others. You should actively listen by asking questions, paying attention to the person talking, and ensuring you're away from distractions, so they feel heard.

Your nonverbal communication is important too, which involves using your body language effectively, maintaining eye contact, using appropriate hand gestures, and altering your tone of voice to reflect the message you're conveying. This is something you can be aware of and develop, in order to improve your communication skills.

A person who is a good communicator is respectful, confident, honest, and communicates with clarity. They have a warm and friendly tone, yet maintain professionalism and this takes practice. You can practice in your personal communication, at work, and at school, so observe how you communicate in different settings!

To develop your communication skills, you should certainly practice, but you should also ask for feedback from your peers. Next time you're sending an email, or calling someone, ask another person to observe and provide feedback. Experience, practice, and feedback are the keys to success!

Other ways to excel at work include:

- Helping someone else when you can—for example, if a colleague is struggling to finish a task and you've completed yours, offer to help out. You could even ask your boss if there are any extra roles or responsibilities they want you to take on.

- Being a team player—this is important, so always do your part and give credit where credit is due. If you're congratulated for completing a task and your colleague has helped you, let everyone know it was a team effort.

- Creating good relationships and impressions—it's important to develop good relationships at work, and first impressions count, so be your authentic self. Show your dependability, honesty, and ability to be helpful and friendly. People will only approach you if you're approachable!

- Creating healthy boundaries—while you want to create a good impression, don't become the "yes" person. If you have your own tasks to complete, explain to your colleagues that you can't help them with their tasks until your own are completed. Learn how to say "no" respectfully by being assertive, yet empathetic to their situation.

- Networking—if you network with others, you'll build connections and people will start to recognize and know you. Having a network at work can open up opportunities for you in the future.

- Leadership skills—there's often a skills gap when it comes to moving from a regular role to a leadership role, so if you want to fast-track your career or gain a promotion, it's important to develop your leadership skills. Taking on more responsibilities, such as offering to lead projects, work shadowing, chairing team meetings, and showing your initiative, are great ways to develop your leadership skills. You can also speak to your manager about what courses they would recommend to help you develop your skills in this area. Look at the job description of a leader within your organization and check out the required skills and experience. Make a self-development plan to gain those skills and experiences.

Working at Home—Top Nine Tips

Sometimes, our job roles require us to work from home. But that isn't always easy, because we are faced with many distractions. If you do need to work from home, here are some tips to help you stay on track:

1. Set some goals—what do you want to achieve today or this week? Be sure to set deadlines!
2. Write a task list of everything you need to do to achieve those goals.
3. Create a schedule based on your task list—make sure you allow enough time per task, and include plenty of breaks throughout the day.
4. Get dressed—sometimes, we just want to stay in our pajamas, so get dressed as if you're really going to work.
5. Shut off your distractions—turn off notifications (you can check your cell phone on your break time), shut off the TV, put on some background music if it helps you focus, and ensure your workspace is clutter-free.

6. If you start to feel tired or lack energy, go for a brisk walk or do some light exercise during your break.

7. Stay hydrated by ensuring plenty of drinks, especially water, are available to you.

8. Check off your to-do list as you achieve each task.

9. Reward yourself for your hard work—this could be with a snack, a movie later, coffee from the local coffee house, or a few minutes playing your favorite mobile game.

Activity #6: SWOT

SWOT simply refers to your:

- Strengths—the things you're good at.
- Weaknesses—the things you need to work on.
- Opportunities—the positive things you can utilize to help you gain an advantage.
- Threats—the barriers that could stand in the way of you achieving your goals.

When you're developing your career, it's important to be able to assess your own skills and abilities. This means knowing your strengths and weaknesses, so you can consider how you can develop further and grow.

One way to do this is to complete a SWOT analysis with your career in mind. Once you master the SWOT analysis, you can apply it to your educational goals and your personal goals, as well as your career. You can even use it to analyze a business idea if you want to set up your own business.

It's your turn to complete a SWOT analysis:

What is your chosen career?
Be sure to research the job description of the career you're interested in, so you know what's required of you.

Strengths	Weaknesses
What do you excel at? What do you do well? What do other people tell you you're good at? What do you do regularly and enjoy?	What could you improve on? What do you feel you don't do well? Is there anything you do that others give you advice in relation to? What do you dislike or avoid doing?
Opportunities	**Threats**
What opportunities are there for you in your chosen career? Are there promotion opportunities, and if so, what? What resources or assets are available to help you achieve your chosen career or a promotion?	What barriers could you face when striving toward your chosen career or a promotion? Do any of your weaknesses make you vulnerable? Who else would want your career—who's your competition? Is there anything outside your control that could prevent your progress?

CHAPTER 7

Choose Your Health

I have chosen to be happy because it is good for my health.

–VOLTAIRE

If you truly want to adult like a pro, you need to ensure you have access to good quality healthcare. This is why this chapter is focused on your personal health and the different choices you have when it comes to health plans and insurance.

In addition to this, we'll focus on how to register with healthcare professionals, while also talking through how to deal with a medical emergency. We'll talk through what you need in your medical kit, and when you should go to the doctor or visit the emergency room (ER). Finally, we're to talk through some CPR basics, as this is an important skill that could save lives.

Don't worry, this chapter won't be too heavy—we're going to make it really quick and easy to follow. Health, after all, is happiness.

Personal Health

Healthcare insurance depends on many different factors, so it isn't always easy to understand. The information in this section will help you develop an understanding of this, but it's important to speak to your insurance provider if you have any questions, as all insurance plans are different.

There are three main types of health insurance available in the US:

1. Health Maintenance Organization (HMO)

This type of insurance means you have a primary care doctor, and if you need specialist treatment, you are referred to them within this network too. This type of policy means that you have to visit doctors within the network, otherwise you will have to pay out-of-network fees yourself.

2. Preferred Provider Organization (PPO)

This is probably the most popular standard insurance plan. It does allow you to use other doctors or healthcare professionals, but it prefers you to use the ones that are part of their network, in order to get a more cost-effective service. External healthcare providers who are not part of the network will likely cost more. You usually do not need a referral to see a specialist.

3. Health Savings Account (HSA)

When you have a health savings account, you are able to save a specific amount of money towards your medical costs. The money will be pre-taxed, and you can access this using a debit card, which is provided by your insurance company. You can use this to buy medical supplements, medical supplies, and vitamins, for example. Money in an HSA can also be invested.

Your insurance plan provider will provide you with a medical card in case an emergency occurs, and this lists information about your plan and coverage.

You must note that insurance does not always cover 100% of your medical bills. For instance, you may be required to pay $500 (or more) towards your treatment before you can claim insurance. They may also cover only 75% of your bill, which means you have to pay for the other 25%. These are known as deductibles, and they will be detailed in your policy. Always read through your insurance policies and the terms of your health plan, and question anything you are unsure of.

A private healthcare plan will cover preventable care, which can stop you from developing medical conditions or prevent them from worsening. This can include immunizations, medical or physical assessments, and any other relevant screenings advised by your doctor.

If a US citizen has low income and is unable to afford healthcare, they would need to apply for Medicaid or the Children's Health Insurance Program (CHIP). Whether you are able to claim this depends on your age, the number of people in your household, if you have a disability or are pregnant, and your income level. You have to apply for this through your local Medicaid agency in the state you live in.

Most employers also offer health plans or insurance as a perk for their full-time employees. You can ask your employer if they offer anything like this, but make sure you read the terms and policy carefully to ensure you know what and who is covered. You can then determine if you still require insurance in addition to this, or you could speak to your insurance company directly with any questions you have. It's worth a conversation, as you could find you're paying your own insurance unnecessarily, or that you aren't covered for as much as you first thought.

If you're traveling out of the country, or even out of state, it's worth double-checking where you stand with your health insurance when it comes to travel. Sometimes, your insurance or the company you've booked your travel with will provide a certain level of coverage for traveling. If you're traveling for work purposes, your employer may cover these costs, but before you travel, ensure you're covered. You may need to pay an extra premium; however, it will benefit you in the long term, as medical care can be extremely expensive.

Typically, dental and vision care is not covered as part of an adult's healthcare insurance plan, so be sure to read through your policy and see what exactly you're covered for. If they are not, you may need to sign up for separate plans to cover these things too.

As I said at the start of this section, health insurance is not the easiest thing to understand, so to adult like a pro, you need to ask questions and get this right. Your healthcare depends on it!

Choosing a Primary Care Doctor

If you need to choose a primary care doctor, dentist, or another healthcare professional, you usually need to get in touch with them directly. You should first check your insurance plan to see if there's a list of doctors or hospitals you're able to use. You then may be asked to complete registration forms, and they could even ask you to attend their office to have a physical. You should ensure your doctor has suitable accreditations; however, if they're suggested or recommended by your insurance, it's likely they've checked this already. Make sure they have your up-to-date contact details, in case they need to call you. While you're speaking to them, it's also your opportunity to ask them any questions you have, especially if you require long-term care.

Once you've chosen your healthcare providers, you can call their office for an appointment or to ask any medical-related questions you have.

How to Deal with a Medical Emergency

In this section, we're going to talk through the things you may need in your home emergency kit, and when you should go to the doctor or visit the ER. Finally, we'll focus on CPR basics and first aid.

Your Home Emergency Kit

You're probably wondering what should be included in your home emergency or first aid kit, so we've provided a checklist to make this really easy for you, based on advice from the American Red Cross (CDC, 2021):

- first aid guidebook—this will talk you through how to use the equipment in your kit
- adhesive bandages in assorted sizes
- antiseptic wipes
- a cold compress
- nonlatex gloves (at least two pairs)
- gauze roller bandage
- sterile gauze
- a thermometer
- compress dressings (at least two)
- a roller bandage
- tweezers
- scissors
- antiseptic ointment
- an emergency blanket

Some people choose to include pain relief and antihistamine medication too. You can also add items to your kit based on your needs. For example, a person may choose to have glucose tablets, if they have diabetes.

When to See Your Doctor or Go to Hospital

Sometimes, it's difficult to decide who to see when you're feeling ill. As a general rule, it's always best to call your doctor's office for advice if you have:

- earache, flu, a cold, or sore throat

- back pain, minor eye injuries, or sprains
- headaches, a fever, a rash
- minor burns or cuts
- a regular vaccination or screening requirement

If your doctor isn't available, you may need to seek out an alternative, which can offer you care. This means visiting an urgent care facility or sometimes the ER.

If there is an urgent care facility, and your doctor isn't available, you could go if you have:

- minor sprains
- coughs, colds, flu, or regarding your asthma
- skin problems, lung issues, urinary issues, or other infections
- broken bones or suspected broken bones
- minor burns
- wound care or if you require stitches

It's time to go to the ER if you have a very serious or life-threatening issue, such as:

- symptoms of stroke
- badly broken bones
- seizures or fainting
- chest pains
- bleeding, which is uncontrolled
- shortness of breath

Of course, it's up to you to decide how serious your situation is. There are some occasions where you need to call for emergency help, especially if you think someone has an injury to their head or neck, is choking, severely burnt, having regular seizures or chest pains, has stopped breathing, suffered an electric shock, or is unconscious. In the US, this means you should call 911, and they will provide you with advice and send medical assistance out to you.

If a person stops breathing, the 911 operator will often talk you through how to give CPR until medical help arrives. Knowing how to administer basic CPR is a potentially lifesaving skill.

CPR Basics

CPR is a resuscitation technique used to save lives in some medical emergencies, where a person has stopped breathing or their heartbeat has stopped. To carry this out, untrained, you should:

- Consider your environment—is the person safe?
- If the person is unconscious, tap their shoulder and ask if they're okay to double check.
- Call 911, as they'll be able to guide you through the CPR process, while sending medical help to your location. Listen carefully and answer their questions.
- Ensure the person is laid flat on their back, on a solid surface with their chin tilted up, exposing their neck.
- Kneel next to their neck and shoulders.
- Place the palm of your hand on the center of their chest, between the nipples.
- Keep your elbows straight and position yourself so that your shoulders are directly above your hands.

- Push down into the chest (about two inches), hard, at a rate of 100–120 compressions a minute, but make sure you're allowing the chest to spring back up after each compression.
- Do this until a medical professional arrives, and stay on the phone with 911 throughout.

If you want to know more about CPR, or receiving first aid training, there are courses you can complete that provide you with relevant training or qualifications. This is an excellent life skill to learn, and it will help you stand out to employers, if you put this on your resume.

Activity #7 – Health Knowledge Mini-Quiz

It's time to check your knowledge of Chapter 7.

1. What type of health insurance allows you to use external healthcare professionals, in addition to the healthcare professionals they recommend?

    a. Health Maintenance Organization
    b. Health Savings Account
    c. Preferred Provider Organization
    d. All of the above

2. If you are experiencing chest pains, who can help you?

    a. Your doctor
    b. 911
    c. Urgent care
    d. The ER

3. If you have an earache, who can help you?

    a. Your doctor
    b. 911
    c. Urgent care
    d. The ER

4. Which of the following is NOT recommended for your home emergency kit?

    a. A cold compress
    b. A sterile gauze
    c. A thermometer
    d. Latex gloves

5. If you need to perform CPR, how many chest compressions should you perform per minute?

    a. 60-80
    b. 50-70
    c. 100-120
    d. 90-110

Now that we've talked about health, it's time to focus on you, your well-being and personal development. Next, we're talking about self-care and growth, but first, let's check your quiz answers on the next page.

Quiz Answers for Activity #7

1. What type of health insurance allows you to use external healthcare professionals, in addition to the healthcare professionals they recommend?

   Answer: c. Preferred Provider Organization

2. If you are experiencing chest pains, who can help you?

   Answer: b. 911

3. If you have an earache, who can help you?

   Answer: a. Your doctor

4. Which of the following is NOT recommended for your home emergency kit?

   Answer: d. Latex gloves

5. If you need to perform CPR, how many chest compressions should you perform per minute?

   Answer: c: 100-120

CHAPTER 8

Self-Care and Growth

You are important.

Yes, I'm talking to you!

If you don't look after yourself as an adult, who will? Taking care of yourself is a skill you can learn. Taking care of yourself results in you having more energy and performing better. It allows you to grow.

Self-care is giving the world the best of you, instead of what's left of you.

–KATIE REED

It's important that you believe you're worthy of being cared for. How can you achieve your dreams or be the best version of you, if you don't take care of yourself?

There are some things you can do, in order to take care of yourself. In this chapter, we're going to start you off with the basics, which involve developing a daily routine, including your sleep, diet, and exercise, and we'll also discuss your mental health.

Let's take the first step by developing a daily routine.

Developing a Daily Routine

You've already learned about scheduling and time management in Chapter 4 when we talked about organization skills, and in other chapters too, like Chapter 6. Having a schedule is important. Your daily routine is important in both your personal and professional life, and this can be part of that schedule. While our days aren't always exactly the same, having a routine can help things run much more smoothly.

Only you can decide what you're going to include in your daily or morning routine, because it must work for you. Many people start and end the day in a particular way; for example, they go to bed and wake up at the same time every day. A morning routine can be extremely important, as it can set you up for the day. You should consider:

- drinking a glass of water to hydrate
- journaling and/or meditating
- exercising for 20–30 minutes
- eating breakfast
- showering or bathing
- dressing.

After that, you should keep yourself motivated by planning and preparing for the day ahead. To do this you should:

- Create a to-do list of the things you need to get done today.

- Turn your to-do list into goals—your goals should be SMART (Specific, Measurable, Achievable, Realistic, and Timely).

The idea of having to-do lists and goals is to keep you motivated. Make sure your goals aren't too complex, because if they are, you may need to break them down into smaller steps. You want to be ticking off the steps on your list, so don't set yourself up to fail.

Now, all you need to do to carry out your daily routine is schedule everything. This includes mealtimes, time spent on social media, and any tasks you have to do at work. When setting up your schedule or daily routine, remember to allow plenty of time for each task and be flexible, as sometimes your priorities have to change, as you respond to events or situations that might come up.

With that in mind, it's important to stay focused, so you can achieve everything you need to achieve. If you need to focus better, you should:

- Eliminate any distractions (close your door, close your windows, turn off notifications, for example).
- Assign a time limit to each task on your to-do list.
- Complete one task at a time—do not multitask.
- Take regular short breaks. This could mean using techniques, such as the Pomodoro technique, which involves working for 25 minutes, before taking a 5-minute break. You set alarms to ensure you take the breaks, and you set short goals of what you want to achieve in the 25-minute period. Go for a walk or meditate to blow off steam and clear your head before you begin a new task.

- Organize your workspace and keep it clutter-free.
- Stay hydrated with water, and have plenty of nutritious snacks at hand that will boost your brain power and energy levels.

Now you've made a start on your daily routine, let's talk through the different ways you can look after yourself and take care of your basic needs.

Look After Yourself

There are five key components of looking after yourself and your needs. These are following a good diet, exercising, sleeping well, having hobbies and interests, and having a social life. Let's explore each of these things.

Following a Good Diet

When we talk about following a good diet, it's basically about using your common sense and eating food that's good for you. We've already talked about cooking on a budget and there are some really healthy and cheap meals that you can make, which are good for you. Plus, it's a lot cheaper to cook for yourself.

To follow a good and healthy diet you should:

- Avoid take-out and junk food.
- Ensure you're eating plenty of fruit and/or vegetables every day.
- Drink at least eight cups of water each day.

It's recommended that the calorie intake for adult men should be 2,200–2,800 per day, and for women, it should be 1800–2,2000 calories per day. It's recommended that these calories are balanced between:

- 45–65% carbohydrates

- 10–35% protein

- 20–35% fat. This includes saturated fats, which should be less than 10%. You should completely avoid trans fats where possible, and instead, you should consume polyunsaturated and monounsaturated fats, as they are the healthier fats. They are available in seeds, fish, vegetable oils, and nuts.

It's important to eat a variety of food as part of a healthy diet, but you do need to ensure you don't consume too much salt or sodium. You should limit your intake of sweets and unhealthy fats as much as you possibly can. Fruit and vegetables should be the main source of your carbohydrate intake, and it's suggested that you have 4½ cups per day. Other dietary recommendations include 3 cups of dairy, 6 ounces of grains, and 6 ounces of meat or beans (Ricketts, 2022).

Maintaining a healthy diet can help you maintain a healthy weight. I'm sure you've heard the saying "you are what you eat," but this could be a good thing, if you keep it healthy. Your diet can have a positive impact on your physical, emotional, and mental health. Exercise can help with that too!

Exercise for Good Health

Exercise is extremely good for you, as it boosts your energy and helps you stay healthy. It's recommended that a person does 150 minutes of moderate exercise each week, such as taking brisk walks each day, biking, or swimming. It's also recommended that you complete strength training around twice per week too, as this can help to condition your body.

Some of the benefits confirmed by Mayo Clinic (2021) include:

- It helps you keep your weight under control.
- It helps to combat health conditions, such as stroke, type 2 diabetes, high blood pressure, metabolic syndrome, anxiety, depression, arthritis, and cancer. It also improves your mental health and cognitive function.
- It boosts your energy levels. When you exercise, it pushes the oxygen around your body and your system speeds up.
- Your mood improves because exercise stimulates brain cells that often leave you feeling happier.
- If you're struggling to sleep, exercise can help you improve this by sleeping more deeply and dropping off faster.

Think

What exercise routine could you create and how much time per week can you dedicate to your physical activities?

There's no getting away from just how beneficial exercise is, and yes, it can certainly improve your sleep, which is why we're going to talk about this in more detail.

Good Sleeping Habits

Getting good sleep isn't always easy, but if you stay committed, you will be able to form some healthy sleeping habits. Having good sleep has a positive impact on mental health, and Suni (2023) suggests that having sufficient sleep allows the brain to evaluate and process emotions more efficiently, whereas lack of sleep can be harmful to the way we consolidate them. He goes on to state how lack of sleep can impact mood and emotions tied to mental health disorders. It's generally recommended that young adults have between 7½–10 hours per night, but sleep is individual, so some people need more than others.

To work out your natural sleeping length, you should monitor your sleep over several occasions without setting an alarm. Note what time you fall asleep, any times you wake up, and when you wake up for good in the morning. Chances are, if you don't wake up for eight hours, that's your natural sleeping pattern. If you wake up in between, it can take a little longer to figure out. Keep going until you can figure out your patterns.

There are some things you can do to improve your ability to sleep and the length of time you sleep. To get into the habit of sleeping well you should:

- Limit your blue light exposure at least an hour before bed.
- Take measures to ensure your bedroom is colder at night, as this helps to encourage sleep.
- Avoid caffeine. Ideally, you shouldn't consume caffeine at least five hours before bed, longer if possible.
- Don't eat too late! As soon as you eat food, it kicks your system into gear.
- Make a playlist of relaxing wind-down music, so you can start to get ready for sleep. If you don't want to listen to music, maybe

try listening to a bed-time story or a guided sleep meditation or hypnosis. Like anything, this is about finding what works for you.

When planning your sleep routine into your schedule, allow plenty of time. An hour before, do something that keeps your attention but switches your focus, like reading a book or writing in your journal.

Start building your routine by determining when you'll sleep, when you'll make up, and how you'll prepare yourself for bed. Sticking to the same sleep and wake times can really help to instill routine.

Hobbies

When creating your daily routine, remember to schedule in some time for your own hobbies and interests. You deserve some me-time, and investing time in yourself is good for building your confidence, self-worth, and self-esteem.

We all have things we like to do, so if you like to draw or color, do that. If you enjoy baking or volunteering, do that. You can shop, sew, write (stories, poetry, articles, or a blog), garden, create games or apps, craft, sculpt, read, dance, ride a bike, or anything else you enjoy doing.

You could even learn a new skill, if you'd like.

Don't be shy when it comes to your hobbies. Embrace them and enjoy!

Create a mind map of your hobbies, including everything you like to do, or things that you're interested in, or want to learn.

You may be surprised by how many things you like.

Social Life—Choosing Your Friends

When you're an adult, you still need a social life and you need people around you whom you know, like, and trust. Our friends are our support network, and they provide influence in our lives, so we want that influence to be positive.

Making friends takes time, and over time, we tend to grow away from certain friends and toward others, and that's because we change too. We often become friends with people whom we have things in common with.

Your social relationships can help reduce stress, because your friends are your biggest supporters and cheerleaders. Your social environment can be very empowering, as having a social network improves your mental and physical health, and it can also help you deal with stress. This encourages you to have positive interactions with others, and helps boost your confidence.

If you have friends with similar interests, it can impact your habits. Some young adults who get a full-time job find that their friends who don't are still in college and stay out late. As a result, you could limit the time you spend with them, as they want you to stay out late too. You may stay out at first, but if it impacts your job, you might decide only to hang with them on the weekend.

When choosing friends, you want to establish relationships with those who will have a positive impact on your life, so you can develop healthy habits and grow.

- Choose friends who have values, hobbies, and interests similar to yours. That way, you can encourage each other.
- Choose friends who are dependable and are willing to support you, guide you, and stand by you.
- Choose wise friends. We want to confide in friends when we need to make important decisions or have a problem, and therefore, we look to our friends to help. Make sure they listen to you, and then ensure you listen to what they say in turn.

It's really difficult to explain how a person should choose friends, because we all have different expectations when it comes to friendships. The most important tip about your social circle and choosing friends is to surround yourself with people who make you feel good. If you're surrounded by negativity, it's time to step away. I'm not saying you don't share bad times with your close friends; however, a friendship is two-sided, so make sure it's not always just about one person. There are good times for both of you, and there are bad times too, which you should share together.

Your Mind

The final part of this chapter covers mental health, because this is such an important topic that we don't talk about enough. Anxiety is extremely common in young adults, yet many people don't even realize they have it.

Anxiety can creep up on you before you know it and symptoms can start off as a churning in your stomach, feelings of restlessness, aches and pains, including headaches, sleep issues, sweating or hot flushes, sick feelings, and a racing heart for no apparent reason.

You could also feel tense or nervous, suffer constant worry, experience feelings of anger or upset, feel down or depressed, have a sense of dread, feelings of disconnect or feel like the world isn't real. Of course, these are not the only symptoms because anxiety is an individual journey for everyone. However, being aware of anxiety can help you spot it as early as possible.

There are many things that cause anxiety (Mind, 2021). When you first move into your own place, you could feel homesick or bogged down by social pressures. There are some ways to combat this, which include:

- Trying to manage your worries by acknowledging them. Write them down and set time aside to focus on them and assess their validity. You can then determine the best cause of action—just be practical!
- Trying breathing exercises—remember, breathe in for four, hold for four, and out for five.
- Talking to someone you trust—talking is important, so if you have any concerns or something is causing you anxiety, talk about it to a friend or family member.
- Trying some complementary therapies to help you relax—this could include reflexology, a massage, hypnotherapy, aromatherapy, or yoga.
- Keeping a diary of your thoughts and feelings. Start logging events and what bothers you, along with how you feel. Can you

notice any early signs when you're triggered? Delve deep into why it's happened, so you can build your awareness.

- Exercising—we've discussed the importance of exercise already, but doing this can certainly help with your mental health too.

Meditation and Mindfulness

Meditation and mindfulness have been mentioned a few times throughout this book, and it's important that you recognize why they're so important. According to Mayo Clinic (2022), they can:

- help you manage stress
- ensure you focus on the present
- increase your self-awareness
- reduce negative emotions
- gain new perspectives when faced with stress
- improve the quality of your sleep
- lower your heart rate
- lower your blood pressure
- increase your imagination
- enhance your creativity
- improve your patience and tolerance levels
- also help manage symptoms of several health conditions, including anxiety.

Meditation is a method that helps you focus and relax by entering a state of awareness. If you're new to meditating, you should:

- Start small—try to meditate between one to five minutes, and then once you get the hang of it, increase your time.
- Focus on your breathing only, and try to switch off from everything else.
- Close your eyes and ensure you're away from distractions or disruptions.
- Notice and acknowledge your thoughts, and then focus back on your breath.
- If you struggle to meditate, try finding a guided meditation or listening to meditation music, such as binaural beats.

Those who meditate regularly report that they have an improved mindset, emotional well-being, memory, and immunity, and are better at managing stress. They also show greater empathy for others, and are generally more positive and content, while being energized enough to focus on the things they really want.

Activity #8: Create Your Morning Routine

Now that you've learned the five key components of taking care of yourself, you're aware of your mental health, and you've considered daily routines, it's time to create your own morning routine.

Focus only on the morning for now.

- What time will you wake up?
- What about exercise and breakfast?
- What about getting dressed?

- Do you have time to journal?
- What are the things you MUST do—your nonnegotiables?

Remember, this schedule is for you, so try to tailor it to your needs!

We've covered so much in this book already, and earlier on, we discussed setting up in your first home. That chapter focused on renting, but next we're going to talk about real estate. It's time to think about buying a property!

CHAPTER 9

....

Buying Your First Home

H ome, sweet home!

There's a sense of accomplishment when you buy your first home. You feel like you've made it, because it's a major life goal for so many people. While owning your home is awesome, there are so many things you need to know and understand before you buy. This will ensure you're fully prepared for the costs, and then the whole process will run smoothly for you.

By knowing these things, you're setting yourself up to win when it comes to buying your own home.

You'll be familiar with some of the things involved with buying your first home, as we'll touch on saving for a house (we mentioned saving in Chapter 3), and then I'll introduce you to the idea of a mortgage, inspections that take place before you buy, inspections that need to take place after you've bought the property, and relevant insurance too.

There's a lot involved when you're considering a mortgage, so it's important to know all the facts. Let's start by defining the term *mortgage* and what it means.

Tell Me About Mortgages

To make this really simple, we're going to briefly discuss what a mortgage is. A mortgage is similar to a loan, but typically it's on a larger scale, because it's a loan to buy a home and the loan is collateral.

The lender charges you interest on the money they lend to you, your lender will then suggest a payment plan, and they then allow you to pay them back, usually while living in the property. If you don't pay, the lender can take the property from you and sell it to make their money back. This is all detailed in the terms and conditions, which is the basis for your contract. You and the mortgage lender sign the contract, as this is a legal agreement between you both.

A person can usually get a mortgage if they are:

- over 18 years old
- have a good credit rating
- have saved a good deposit that is equivalent to 10% or more of the property value. For example, if the property costs $350,000, you would need to save at least $35,000. The bigger your deposit, the more likely you are to get the mortgage. Let's say you saved up $45,000, but the home was $300,000. You'd have a 15% deposit towards the property, and this would impact you positively in the eyes of a lender.

A mortgage can be agreed to be paid back over a long period of time, typically around 25–30 years. However, you can agree to shorter terms if you want to pay it off more quickly. This can impact the interest you are charged by the lender, as this varies between mortgage companies, based on your circumstances and the type of loan. Interest is usually charged on a fixed-rate basis (which means you pay a set amount each month) or an adjustable-rate basis (which means the amount you pay can vary, often in line with interest rates).

Fixed-rate and adjustable-rate are the two most common types of mortgages. However, there are some variations available if you're buying a home for the first time, or if you're a veteran. It's worth speaking to a mortgage broker to find out which mortgage type works best for you. If you want to get the best mortgage, you need to ensure you have a good credit score, using the tips we discussed in Chapter 3.

To apply for a mortgage, it's recommended that you get in touch with a broker, as they can arrange everything for you and help you through the process. They have the best knowledge and keep up-to-date with the market. This is really useful if you're buying your first home.

Your mortgage broker will be able to tell you how much you can borrow. The lender uses affordability and risk to make their decision, which is based on your savings, your income and job security, your financial responsibilities, your debts, and your credit score. This is usually a maximum of three times your income. So, if you earn $42,000 per year, you could potentially borrow a maximum of $126,000, if you were buying alone. However, if you want to buy a home worth $130,000 but you've saved $26,000, and your family is gifting you another $13,000 in addition to that, you'd only need to borrow $91,000. This would look really responsible to your lender, and you'd be more likely to get the loan approved when they consider affordability and risk.

Your mortgage broker will ask you a range of questions and help you get preapproved. To do this, they may need to ask you for proof of your income, bank statements, and proof of identity. This is normal, so be ready to provide as much information as possible to show you're in a secure job, can afford the mortgage payments, and you are a responsible lender.

Mortgage brokers charge you fees, and there are other fees involved in buying a home too. This is something else to consider, as buying a home for the first time can be expensive. Sometimes, there are real estate fees, mortgage fees, legal fees, your deposit, and fees for your broker. You'll have upkeep expenses to pay throughout the duration of owning a home, so if you choose a home that needs renovations or improvements, you need to take this into account as well. In addition to this, you need to pay inspection fees too (we'll talk about this next).

Make sure you're aware of all the additional costs involved in owning your home, so you can make a well-informed decision. It's recommended that you set aside at least one percent of your home's value every year for essential repairs.

Once you have your preapproval and know how much you can borrow, all that's left is for you to choose a property you like.

Home Inspections

Buying a home is expensive, so before you buy it, you should have it checked out by a home inspector. Your home inspector should be a professional, because they're going to look around the home you're about to purchase and consider all the major and minor issues.

A home inspection is often a condition of your mortgage, because if there is faulty wiring, mold, or other major problems, it can impact the value of the home. If this isn't a condition of your mortgage, as it isn't compulsory, it should be, so protect yourself by arranging this. Your mortgage company may not agree to let you borrow the money as a result, because such repairs may make the home riskier, as you may not be able to afford the upkeep. For this reason, it's a critical part of buying the home.

Many people are already locked into a contract when they order a home inspection; however, a contingency is usually agreed on that you have seven days following the inspection to walk away, penalty-free, should there be significant issues. You should ensure this applies to you or you may be stuck paying fees. If this isn't a term of your agreement, you should request that it is.

The home inspector will look at both the interior and exterior of the home, considering things such as plumbing, electric wiring, the roof of the home, the foundation, and much more.

A pre-home inspection will safeguard you in the long term, so it's certainly something you should account for when buying a home. You should ensure that a licensed provider completes this for you and provides you with a written report of their findings.

Some people choose to have further safety inspections done once they've purchased their home too. This looks more in depth at safety in the property and makes recommendations for repairs that will improve the safety of the home. This could be a suggestion of something that needs to be replaced, but is not urgent, like doors and windows, fire alarms or detectors, home security, or even fence repairs.

Relevant Insurance for Homeowners

Insurance can be complicated, so in this section, we're going to look at some things that are applicable to homeowners, such as homeowner's insurance, which covers buildings and contents; life insurance, which pays out on your death and lasts the entirety of your life; and mortgage life insurance, which pays your mortgage in the event of your death, but only lasts for the duration of your mortgage.

Remember, paying insurance means you have to pay extra money!

When you're buying a home, it's important to consider homeowner's insurance, and while this isn't always mandatory, some mortgage providers will only allow you to have your mortgage if you agree to have this.

Homeowner's insurance can include your building and contents, which covers the structures on your property, your personal property, and some even have personal liability, medical payments to others, and costs incurred due to loss of use.

Life insurance is sometimes a stipulation in order to get a mortgage too; however, this isn't always the case. Some financial lenders will try to sell you mortgage life insurance, which means if anything happens to you, your mortgage will be paid. This is only relevant during the time of the mortgage. If you get generic life insurance, which pays as a death benefit, it's worth considering, so you could have enough coverage for your mortgage with some extra left over.

Having extra insurance policies will add to your everyday expenses, so it's a good idea to see if your mortgage broker has any advice regarding the best policies. You can also get quotes online for the different types of insurance. Insurance brokers can also help you choose the best policies and get the best rates, so if you do want insurances to ensure you have good coverage, it's worth exploring further and assessing how much this would cost you and the length of coverage. Some life insurance policies last a lifetime, but other insurance policies simply cover you for a specific number of years or on a yearly basis, and then you renew each year.

Activity #9: Homeowner Research Task

To complete this research task, you need to:

- Look online and find a house you like that's on the market.
- Work out how much you need to be earning in your job to buy that house and how much deposit you should save.
- Research other costs—legal costs, real estate costs, mortgage broker costs, inspection costs, and insurance. Remember to set aside one percent of the home's value each year for repairs.
- Calculate how much you would need to save, in order to buy this house. Many people buy a home with their partner, and while things could change, this can give you a realistic idea of how much you would need to get on the property ladder.

- When can you start saving?

While all this information can feel quite overwhelming, it's important that you know the facts about buying your first home. It requires you to commit to your savings, and in order to do that, you need to make sure you invest your time finding out as much as possible, so you can make informed decisions about your finances and your life.

In the final chapter, we're going to talk about staying safe. Your parents take care of you and remind you regularly to be safe, but when you're an adult, you have to take this on yourself. Being aware of safety issues and measures is important to safeguard and protect yourself.

CHAPTER 10

Staying Safe

Personal safety is such an important topic, because in order to adult like a pro, it's our responsibility to protect ourselves and our property in the best possible way, to prevent security or safety breaches.

Having a basic awareness of safety can really make a difference in your life, and while the aim of this chapter isn't to scare you, it's important that you have good knowledge when it comes to this topic.

There are many ways to stay safe, so by the end of this chapter, you'll be clear on what it means to be safe and secure. You'll recognize these things already, but when we're adulting, knowing is not enough, it's time to take control.

You're about to explore personal safety, and how you can make your property secure too. We'll consider locks on your doors and windows, CCTV, walking alone at night, and personal safety measures to keep you safe. We'll also explore e-safety, as this is another important issue, because of things like fraud, scams, and staying safe on social media.

Let's start by talking about staying secure in the home. Home should be your safe haven!

Ten Tips for Staying Secure at Home

To stay secure at home, there are measures you can take. These include:

- Having a security system and alarms to increase the security of your home.

- Making sure your entry doors are secure and they have two locks.

- Getting lockable windows so you can secure them when you're in bed or not home.

- Having security lights in your yard and a porch light, so you can go outside when it's dark. Security lights that come on with a sensor are a good deterrent for unwanted visitors and you can always use solar-powered lights too.

- Using security or CCTV cameras. You can get doorbells that have security cameras now, and CCTV can be motion-activated so that it records when there is motion outside your home.

- Making your space open, and eliminating hiding places, where people can hide out of view or from security cameras. All sheds and gates should have locks too.

- Automating your home. For example, scheduling the lights to turn on and off if you're on vacation or out for a long time. Use smart doorbells too. Some people have the ability to check on fire and carbon monoxide alarms inside the home too, and cancel them if it's a false alarm.

- Making sure your fire alarms or detectors are checked on a yearly basis, and ensuring you can make your escape in the event of a fire. Some people choose to invest in fire extinguishers for the kitchen area too, as this is a common area for a fire.

- Securing your garage, especially if it leads directly into the home. Make sure any internal-leading doors are extra secure, preferably with two locks. Install smart garage door openers and secure the garage door with extra locks. Your garage can also be alarmed along with your house and be automated as well.

- Getting a safe for your valuables. If you have anything that's worth a lot of money or is personal, such as a passport, it's good to have a steel safe, and you can even get them installed in a hidden place, such as under the floor or within a wall. Look for safes that have two locks for security reasons.

Walking Alone at Night Safely

It's really important that you stay safe when walking at night. Of course, it's suggested that you avoid this completely, but this isn't always possible. Therefore, it's time to explore some safety tips:

- Stick to well-lit areas.
- Try to stick to main streets with streetlights. Don't take short cuts down dark roads or alleyways, if possible.
- Check in with friends and family. Let them know when you're walking home and what route you're taking.

- Install find-me apps, so someone you trust can track your route.
- Carry a personal alarm that makes a loud noise if you're in danger.

It can be a tricky situation if you have to walk alone at night, so it is better to find someone to walk with, get a ride with someone you know, take public transport, or call a cab or Uber, if possible. Your safety is extremely important, so be cautious and watch out for possible dangers and risks.

Now, let's turn to e-safety.

E-Safety—Staying Safe Online

Online crimes are becoming increasingly prevalent, so as an adult, you need to be aware of all the risks you face. There are so many convincing frauds and scams out there, it can be difficult to spot them at first. You have to raise your awareness.

When you put your details into a website to buy something online, you could be at risk of fraud and identity theft. If you receive an email that appears to be from your bank and it wants you to click a link and input your details, that's also likely to be a scam, because someone wants your bank details and internet passwords.

When we're young, it seems like a good idea to check ourselves in on social media, but that can pose a risk. If you're on vacation as an adult who lives alone, you're at risk of making your home a target for burglary.

Let's talk about some of the key online scams you may encounter as you enter young adulthood.

Online Shopping Safety

When you shop online, you are often expected to share personal details about yourself, which can make you vulnerable to identity theft and fraud. Identity theft is when someone uses your name and personal information to get access to loans and credit, which they then don't pay back. Because it's in your name, you can be held liable and it can reflect poorly on your credit profile. Obviously, there are ways to sort this out, but it's a criminal investigation that takes time. Fraud is similar, as this is when a person deceives others, in order to gain financially or in a personal capacity.

Let's say you place an order for an item of clothing. You put in your name, your delivery address, your contact number, your payment card address, your card details, and sometimes, you have to put in your date of birth too. If a scammer gets hold of these details, you're certainly at risk of fraud and identity theft. To stay safe when shopping online, you should:

- Ensure you have good antivirus and firewall software installed. Some people opt to have a VPN too, which ensures their network stays private.
- Shop with reputable retailers you know and trust, and be sure to vet businesses you are new to using. Look them up and pay attention to the details. One single typing error is sometimes difficult to notice, but sometimes the scammer opens a site with

one letter or number extra or different—so always pay close attention to those details.

- Avoid using public Wi-Fi to shop, opt for private instead. People can use a public network to hack into your device and gain your personal information.

- Use strong passwords that have numbers, symbols, and letters—preferably something really random. Avoid names and other obvious words or number sequences.

- Check the website's security before you buy. Sites that are protected by SSL have a lock icon in the navigation bar and start with 'https' rather than just 'http'. 'Https' indicates a secure website.

- A shopping website will not need your Social Security number, so do not give that out!

- Paying via a credit card can protect you, as this does not give others direct access to your bank account. Credit cards often offer fraud protection, so you can call them if you believe you're a victim.

- Some card issuers allow you to use a temporary virtual credit card, so you're not putting your actual details into the website.

- Always check your statements and transactions to ensure there's nothing suspicious.

Phishing or Email Scams

Sometimes, you get emails or text messages offering great deals, telling you that you've missed a delivery, or telling you that you need to update your password because you've been identified as being at risk of fraud.

Generally, messages like these are trying to scam or defraud you. If you receive messages like these, always check out the sender. They will try and make you believe they are from specific companies, but it's always best not to click and follow links or open downloads unless you are absolutely sure. If you do, they could infect your device with viruses and malware that will help a hacker spy on you and obtain your information.

Always report, block, and delete such messages!

Social Media Safety

We've talked a little already about social media safety and how checking ourselves in online can be a mistake or put you at risk, but there's so much more to social media safety. You've probably heard that there is a lot of bullying online, and if you don't protect yourself, you could be vulnerable to this.

It's a good idea to go into your social media settings and check your privacy settings, so only the people you want can see your information. You should only add people to your network if you are sure you know, like, and trust them. If you add someone you think you know, and they make you feel uncomfortable or upset, just delete and block them.

It's important to be cautious when online, because there is so much fake news and misinformation. Don't just believe everything you read. Check it out externally by using search engines to research what you've heard, and you can see if there is any substance to what you've been told.

Remember, social media isn't good for your mental health, due to all the misinformation and bullying. If you're being cyberbullied or trolled, this can have a huge impact on you. Take a break when you need to, and if you are being trolled or cyberbullied, report this. If you put a lot of private information or images on social media, it's possible for trolls, bullies, and hackers to get information they can use against you. Don't give them the opportunity and be clever about what content you share. If things get out of hand online, it can become a police matter, so speak to someone about this (a friend or family member) and see what they think you should do. There are lots of advice websites out there that can help you deal with such situations, so you're not alone.

It's time to act against online crime and bullying and enforce internet safety. It should be an inclusive environment for all, so let's make sure we take action to make sure of this!

Activity #10: Reflection

For the final activity in the book, you should take the opportunity to reflect on your safety, and consider what you would do in specific situations:

- You've just moved into a new apartment. The outside area and entry hall have CCTV, motion-sensor lights, and a security guard watches over the reception area at night. What three security measures would you put in place to protect your property (the apartment itself)?

- You're walking home from a bar late at night, as you couldn't get a cab. You only live five blocks away, but one of the streets is dark and quiet, and several people have been robbed there. How do you approach this situation? What would you do?

- Someone who used to bully you in school is trying to add you on social media. You left school five years ago and are hoping that things have changed, but you're not sure. You don't want to leave yourself in a vulnerable position. What would you do?

- You've got an email from a company you've recently ordered from, saying they can't process your order because they need you to provide your card details again by clicking the link. The money is already showing as pending from your credit card account, but you really want the items. How would you check if the email was legitimate?

There are no set right or wrong answers here, it's simply about using the information you've learned and applying it to real-life situations. The most important thing is to keep you safe and increase your awareness of personal safety.

Remember,

When safety is first, you last.

–UNKNOWN

Stay safe!

CONCLUSION

You've made it to the end of the book and you're ready to be an adult. Adulting is serious business; however, that doesn't mean it can't also be fun. Learning the valuable adulting life skills in this book can be the key to your success—it's your path toward *adulting like a pro*!

Throughout this book, we've explored your passions, talked about money and how to build good money habits, and considered how to find, source, and keep a home, regardless of whether you are renting or buying. In fact, we've talked about finances, contracts, and legalities in both cases. We've even discussed everyday skills, such as cooking, ironing, budgeting, and shopping. These are all key life skills.

Many adults have a car, but if you have a car, you need to take care of it, so we've covered this too, as often, owning a car can help with your career as well. While your personal life is important, this book also covers work and the skills you need to find a job and get a promotion, because if you want to be a successful adult, your career is important!

We go through our childhood, and typically, our parents or caretakers tend to take care of us, but when you're adulting, you have to take care of yourself. You'll be able to do that comfortably now that we've discussed personal health and health plans, along with self-care and personal growth. We've also covered keeping yourself safe, as this is another responsibility of an adult that helps you adult like a true pro.

Now that you're equipped with the essential knowledge and skills you need, you can enjoy the journey into adulthood. As an adult, you're in charge of your own destiny, and it's time for you to take the reins.

Learning to be an adult may seem overwhelming, as there are a lot of instructions to follow, but when we break everything down into small steps, it becomes easier and more achievable, which was the aim of this book.

While it may seem daunting to have to do all the chores around the house, manage money, pay bills and taxes, maintain a job and a social life, as well as looking after your personal health and safety, it's something you can't avoid. Using the tools, hacks, and tips explained in this book can make that whole transition into adulthood easier.

The things you learned in this book aren't a secret, they're things commonly discussed, but you just need to keep practicing and mastering the skills you've learned.

There's no time like the present.

- Start by looking around your room and see how you can make it tidier and more organized.
- Speak to your parents and ask them which chores they are happy to assign you.
- Look for a part-time job and start saving your money.

- What about your social environment? Do your friends bring out the best in you? Do they encourage you to develop good habits or push you into making the wrong decisions?

Making conscious choices and decisions is a part of adult life, and this is your cue to start preparing for success in adulthood. Rest assured, when it's done right; it IS a great time to live. So, enjoy it.

It's time to live your best life!

Before you head off and put what you've learned into full flow, please leave a review of this book. I'd love to know what your favorite part was and how you plan on implementing what you've learned.

I want to leave you with one last thought:

Don't go through life, grow through life.

–ERIC BUTTERWORTH

REFERENCES

Anxiety signs and symptoms. (2021, February). Mind.
https://www.mind.org.uk/information-support/types-of-mental-
health-problems/anxiety-and-panic-
attacks/symptoms/?gclid=CjwKCAiA0JKfBhBIEiwAPhZXD8t7n4V
cqN_qH-T-Y71KtC9cimtHTCX9oTPjylFK0-
NYiq5kCevejRoCmw0QAvD_BwE

Bank of America. (2019). Creating a budget with a personal budget
spreadsheet. Better Money Habits.
https://bettermoneyhabits.bankofamerica.com/en/saving-
budgeting/creating-a-budget

Blog Administrator. (2021, May 13). Must-haves for your first-aid kit.
Center for Disease Control.
https://blogs.cdc.gov/publichealthmatters/2021/05/first-aid-kits/

Bloomenthal, A. (2022, June 14). Why you don't need mortgage life
insurance. Investopedia.
https://www.investopedia.com/mortgage/insurance/why-you-dont-
need-mpli/

Business communication and technology: How tech can grow your business.
(2021, October 27). Grammarly Business.
https://www.grammarly.com/business/learn/business-
communication-and-
technology/?&utm_source=bing&utm_medium=cpc&utm_campai

gn=384891503&utm_targetid=dat-2332820076896030:loc-188&msclkid=05ecef19fa771b98b2e78ccc5e918eae&gclid=05ecef19fa771b98b2e78ccc5e918eae&gclsrc=3p.ds

Buying a car in the USA. (n.d.). The American Dream. https://www.the-american-dream.com/buying-a-car-in-the-usa/

Can't decide where to go for care? Call your doctor's office first. (n.d.). Trihealth. https://www.trihealth.com/dailyhealthwire/miscellaneous/should-i-go-to-my-doc-or-the-er

Carol. (2023, January 25). How to maintain a clutter free home - 7 simple tips. My Tidy Corner. https://www.mytidycorner.com/how-to-maintain-a-clutter-free-home/#:~:text=How%20to%20Maintain%20a%20Clutter%20Free%20Home%20%E2%80%93

Cerball, A. (2020, March 1). Quotes for living your best life: 80 motivational quotes. Alex Cerball. https://alexcerball.com/quotes-on-living-your-best-life/

Chan, J., & Ellerby, D. (2022, July 20). The 5 best laundry detergents you can buy. USA TODAY. https://eu.usatoday.com/story/tech/reviewedcom/2022/07/20/5-best-laundry-detergents-you-can-buy/10111833002/

Cherry, K. (2021, July 15). 5 surprising ways to increase motivation. Verywell Mind. https://www.verywellmind.com/surprising-ways-to-get-motivated-2795388

Cherry, K. (2022, September 8). How meditation impacts your mind and body. Verywell Mind. https://www.verywellmind.com/what-is-meditation-2795927#toc-how-to-practice-meditation

Clissitt, C. (2020, February 20). 7 tips for job hunting in the USA. MoveHub. https://www.movehub.com/au/moving-overseas/usa/job-hunting/

Content Team. (2019, May 20). How to write a job advert (with examples). Recruitment Insight. https://www.cv-library.co.uk/recruitment-insight/write-job-advert-with-examples/

Cornerstone. (2021, December 6). The best personal SWOT analysis examples for students. Cornerstone International Community College of Canada. https://ciccc.ca/blog/career-in-canada/swot-analysis-examples-students/

Dahl, D. (2022, September 3). 50 stay safe quotes to keep you healthy and well. Everyday Power. https://everydaypower.com/50-stay-safe-quotes-to-keep-you-healthy-and-well/

Dean, A. (2019, June 11). Looking for a home to rent? Real Homes. https://www.realhomes.com/advice/viewing-a-rental-property-10-essentials-to-look-out-for

Dean, A. (2022, August 10). Looking for a new place to rent? Real Homes. https://www.realhomes.com/advice/questions-to-ask-a-landlord-before-renting

Doster, N. (2019, February 12). 150 freezer meal recipes. Taste of Home; Taste of Home. https://www.tasteofhome.com/collection/freezer-meal-recipes/

Dungy, T. (2018, August 3). 3 things to remember when choosing friends. All pro Dad. https://www.allprodad.com/3-things-to-remember-when-choosing-friends/

Eads, A. (2023, January 11). How to find your passion for a more fulfilling career. Indeed Career Guide. https://www.indeed.com/career-advice/finding-a-job/how-to-find-your-passion

Edwards, R. (2020, October 15). 10 simple ways to secure your new home. SafeWise. https://www.safewise.com/blog/10-simple-ways-to-secure-your-new-home/

Fennell, A. (2021, March 12). How long recruiters spend looking at your CV | 2023 study. StandOutCV. https://standout-cv.com/how-long-recruiters-spend-looking-at-cv#:~:text=Key%20CV%20statistics&text=80%25%20of%20CVs%20do%20not

Find doctors and medical facilities. (n.d.). USA.gov. https://www.usa.gov/doctors

Finding your passion quotes. (n.d.). Ellevate Network. Retrieved February 25, 2023, from https://www.ellevatenetwork.com/articles/7851-quotes-about-finding-your-passion?gaaction=user+created&gacategory=acquisition&galabel=o auth&galabel=oauth_onetap&modal=join

Fire safety tips. (n.d.). Safe Kids Worldwide. https://www.safekids.org/tip/fire-safety-tips#:~:text=Be%20Aware%20of%20Fire%20Hazards%20in%20You r%20Home

Fontinelle, A. (2022, August 12). Importance of home inspection contingency. Investopedia. https://www.investopedia.com/articles/mortgages-real-estate/08/home-inspection.asp

Godwin, J. (2021, March 18). 7 tips for a good night's sleep. The Pulse Blog. https://ouraring.com/blog/7-sleep-tips-for-better-sleep/

Herbert, J. (2021). 5 surprising benefits of being organized. Select Health. https://selecthealth.org/blog/2021/01/5-surprising-benefits-of-being-organized

How much house can I afford? | How much can I borrow? (n.d.). US Bank. https://www.usbank.com/home-loans/mortgage/first-time-home-buyers/how-much-house-can-i-afford.html

How to change a tyre in 10 simple steps. (2018, June 25). RAC. https://www.rac.co.uk/drive/advice/car-maintenance/how-to-change-a-tyre/

How to file your federal taxes. (n.d.). USA.gov. https://www.usa.gov/file-taxes

Indeed Editorial Team. (2023, January 31). What is a side hustle? (plus 15 ideas for making extra money). Indeed Career Guide. https://www.indeed.com/career-advice/finding-a-job/what-is-side-hustle

Johansen, A. G. (2020, November 11). 15 tips for safer online shopping. LifeLock by Norton. https://lifelock.norton.com/learn/internet-security/safe-online-shopping

Kagan, J. (2021, February 25). Mortgage. Investopedia. https://www.investopedia.com/terms/m/mortgage.asp

Kearns, D. (2022, June 21). How to choose the best mortgage for you. Investopedia. https://www.investopedia.com/mortgage/mortgage-guide/how-to-choose-best-mortgage/

Kislitsyna, M. (2018, May 17). Extensive List of First Apartment Essentials For Renters. Tenants Blog - Rentberry. https://rentberry.com/blog/first-rental-essentials

Kurtuy, A. (n.d.). Top 10 communication skills (for your life & career). Novorésumé. https://novoresume.com/career-blog/communication-skills

Lauren, A. (2021, February 27). How to decorate your first apartment or home. Forbes. https://www.forbes.com/sites/amandalauren/2021/02/27/how-to-decorate-your-first-apartment-or-home/?sh=57c6e0c72cd1

Layte, R. (n.d.). The powerful effect of your social environment. FutureLearn. Retrieved February 25, 2023, from https://www.futurelearn.com/info/courses/successful-ageing/0/steps/11842

Life skills - laundry. (n.d.). Revelle College US San Diego. https://revelle.ucsd.edu/res-life/life-skills/laundry.html#Washing

Maintaining Your Vehicle. (2021, April 1). The ultimate car maintenance checklist. Www.bridgestonetire.com. https://www.bridgestonetire.com/learn/maintenance/ultimate-car-maintenance-checklist/#

Mayo Clinic. (2021, October 8). 7 great reasons why exercise matters. Mayo Clinic. https://www.mayoclinic.org/healthy-lifestyle/fitness/in-depth/exercise/art-20048389

Mayo Clinic. (2022, February 12). Cardiopulmonary resuscitation (CPR): First aid. Mayo Clinic. https://www.mayoclinic.org/first-aid/first-aid-cpr/basics/art-

20056600#:~:text=Cardiopulmonary%20resuscitation%20(CPR)%2
0is%20a

Mayo Clinic Staff. (2020, April 22). A beginner's guide to meditation. Mayo
     Clinic. https://www.mayoclinic.org/tests-procedures/meditation/in-
     depth/meditation/art-20045858

McDonough, L. S. (2020, March 13). How to DIY an all-purpose cleaner
     that actually works. Good Housekeeping.
     https://www.goodhousekeeping.com/home/cleaning/tips/a24885/m
     ake-at-home-cleaners/

Mitchell, S. (n.d.). How to care for a steam iron. Home Guides | SF Gate.
     Retrieved February 25, 2023, from
     https://homeguides.sfgate.com/care-steam-iron-20252.html

Morin, A. (2020, July 13). 7 ways to find more meaning and purpose in your
     life. Verywell Mind. https://www.verywellmind.com/tips-for-
     finding-your-purpose-in-life-4164689

Page, S. (2021, February 8). 27 inspirational health quotes to motivate
     employees. Total Wellness Health.
     https://info.totalwellnesshealth.com/blog/27-inspirational-health-
     quotes

Parade. (2020, January 21). 150 life quotes — inspiring the happy, good and
     funny in life. Parade; Parade.
     https://parade.com/937586/parade/life-quotes/

Real Simple Editors. (2023, February 3). The ultimate cleaning checklist.
     Real Simple. https://www.realsimple.com/home-
     organizing/cleaning/house-cleaning-
     schedule#:~:text=The%20Ultimate%20Cleaning%20Checklist%201
     %20Daily%20Make%20your

Ricketts, D. (2022). Nutrition needs during adulthood. Study.com. https://study.com/academy/lesson/nutrition-needs-during-adulthood.html#:~:text=It%20is%20recommended%20that%20adults

Scott, S. J. (2019, July 22). What is your why? 12 steps to find your purpose in life. Develop Good Habits. https://www.developgoodhabits.com/your-why/#:~:text=It%20allows%20you%20to%20live%20a%20life%20with

Should I get a car? The pros and cons of car ownership. (2018, March 16). First Insurance Company of Hawaii. https://www.ficoh.com/info-center/lets-talk-first/should-i-get-a-car-the-pros-and-cons-of-car-ownership/#:~:text=Pros%3A%20Cars%20are%20associated%20with

Social media advice hub. (n.d.). Internet Matters. https://www.internetmatters.org/resources/social-media-advice-hub/?gclid=CjwKCAiAlp2fBhBPEiwA2Q10D4xadTHoxpEFK8vc4PaSaLrPdG0jxewoGQyvoLC-qNidfEz4okArmRoCnlEQAvD_BwE

Stahl, A. (2020, October 13). How to turn your side hustle into full-time business. Forbes. https://www.forbes.com/sites/ashleystahl/2020/10/13/how-to-turn-your-side-hustle-into-full-time-business/?sh=43e0ac17b1a0

Strehlow, R. N. (2020, March 12). Working from home: 10 tips for ultimate productivity. Wix Blog. https://www.wix.com/blog/2020/03/working-from-home-tips/?utm_source=google&utm_medium=cpc&utm_campaign=13774768257%5e126077909722&experiment_id=%5e%5e53169981406 7%5e%5e_DSA&gclid=Cj0KCQiA54KfBhCKARIsAJzSrdoYd5TV80cBh3ev4BTVe8zHB5WrqdLDX4ZxjOFCUsCK399e1cnF6ioaAru WEALw_wcB

Stych, A. (2019, July 26). Here's when workers are the most productive. Bizwomen the Business Journals. https://www.bizjournals.com/bizwomen/news/latest-news/2019/07/heres-when-workers-are-the-mostproductive.html?page=all#:~:text=Morning%20is%20the%20best%20time

Sundar, S. (2023, February 1). If you still aren't sure what ChatGPT is, this is your guide to the viral chatbot that everyone is talking about. Business Insider. https://www.businessinsider.com/everything-you-need-to-know-about-chat-gpt-2023-1?r=US&IR=T#:~:text=Chat%20bots%20like%20GPT%20are

Suni, E. (2020, September 18). Mental health and sleep. Sleep Foundation. https://www.sleepfoundation.org/mental-health#:~:text=Sufficient%20sleep%2C%20especially%20REM%20sleep

Team Tony. (n.d.). 12 tips on finding your purpose in life | TonyRobbins. Tony Robbins. https://www.tonyrobbins.com/stories/date-with-destiny/what-is-my-purpose/

Top 10 study skills. (n.d.). University of Lynchburg. https://www.lynchburg.edu/academics/tutoring-and-academic-support/top-10-study-skills/

US car insurance. (n.d.). Clements. Retrieved February 25, 2023, from https://www.clements.com/personal/international-car-insurance/usa/

When to go to the ER, urgent care or your doctor? (n.d.). MDVIP. https://www.mdvip.com/about-mdvip/blog/should-you-go-er-urgent-care-or-your-primary-care-doctor

Wise. (2017, August 24). *American mortgages and home loans: A foreigner's guide*. Wise. https://wise.com/gb/blog/getting-a-mortgage-in-usa#:~:text=The%20step%2Dby%2Dstep%20process

You have health insurance, but what about vision and dental insurance? (2022, June 14). Health Markets. https://www.healthmarkets.com/resources/supplemental-health-insurance/health-insurance-vision-dental-insurance/

Your resume: What to put in, what to leave out. (n.d.). Columbia University Center for Career Education. Retrieved February 25, 2023, from https://www.careereducation.columbia.edu/resources/your-resume-what-put-what-leave-out

THANK YOU

Thank you for your purchase. If you enjoyed this book, we would highly appreciate it if you could leave a review on Amazon. Your feedback is invaluable as it motivates the author. We'd love to know what your favorite part of the book was.

It only takes 5 seconds and helps small businesses like ours.

Go to this link:

http://amazon.com/review/create-review?&asin=B0C2S277ZL

Or simply scan the following QR code:

Regards,
Miranda Young

Made in United States
Troutdale, OR
06/05/2024

20349025R00089